"Paul's definitive declaration on church life is found in the book of Ephesians—life through, from, in, with, for, and under the Lord Jesus Christ, the Son of God and Savior of sinners, the Redeemer, risen, reigning, and returning, now and henceforth forever, by the Father's appointment, Lord of all. The whole of this comes into focus in Gloria Furman's applicatory overview of Ephesians, which I enthusiastically commend as vitamin-packed nourishment for Christians everywhere."

J. I. Packer, Board of Governors' Professor of Theology, Regent College

"Some expositions are careful, line-by-line, evenhanded explanations of the biblical text. This exposition is exuberant, irrepressible, and intoxicating. Its strength is that its author, Gloria Furman, has tasted for herself the bliss of being loved by God, and she wants her readers to drink deeply from the same fountain."

D. A. Carson, Research Professor of New Testament, Trinity Evangelical Divinity School; Cofounder, The Gospel Coalition

"*Alive in Him* brings together the rich reality of both the transcendence and immanence of life in Christ. The truths found within its pages remind us that relationship must always precede response. But when that relationship is rooted in the 'riches of his grace,' that treasure transforms every other relationship."

Karen Hodge, Coordinator for Women's Ministry, Presbyterian Church in America; author, *Transformed: Life-taker to Life-giver*

"This is a wonderfully heartwarming overview of Ephesians that will encourage and inspire even the most weary of saints. Gloria has worked hard to show how Paul's letter fits into the bigger picture of God's revelation and writes in a way that makes these foundational truths both accessible and digestible. Each chapter helps us to join the dots of God's great plan of salvation that is bringing all things together under the lordship of Christ. With well-worked illustrations and realistic applications, this book challenged me again and again to delight in the love of God and its transforming power so that I might become more like Chris^t ~~~~~ l~~~~ ~~~~~~ greater glory."

Carrie Sandom, Director of W~~ Associate Minister for Women *Different by Design: God's Bl~

D0170348

"Reading *Alive in Him* was like sitting down to a beautiful, soul-nourishing meal, hosted by a good friend. Gloria packs each chapter full of rich truths from Ephesians, and you can't help but be swept up into her enthusiasm for God's Word and the gospel story. Gloria is especially skilled at lifting our eyes up from out of the weeds to see the bigger picture: the glorious reality of being 'alive in Christ' and what that means to our every day. Accessible, faithful, full of contagious exuberance and joy, and rich with nourishment for your soul, I highly recommend this book."

Caroline Cobb, singer-songwriter

"*Alive in Him* is engaging, refreshing, and marvelously surefooted. A delightful read!"

J. Gary Millar, author, *Now Choose Life: Theology and Ethics in Deuteronomy* and *Calling on the Name of the Lord*

"In the best possible way, *Alive in Him* is an unusual book. It is not a commentary, atomizing and analyzing each word and verse. It is not asking the reader to pick a side in a contentious current debate. It is not a greeting card–type devotional that reduces the biblical text to pious platitudes. Rather, it is an in-depth reflection on Ephesians that, in style and content, captures Paul's bounding enthusiasm in that letter for the majesty of Christ and his gospel and asks us to respond in wonder and praise to God."

Claire Smith, Bible teacher; author, *God's Good Design: What the Bible Really Says about Men and Women*

"Ephesians 4 tells us, 'He gave some as teachers, for the equipping of the saints for the work of service, to the building up of the body of Christ.' I am deeply grateful that God gave Gloria Furman to the church. Because geography separates us, I can count on one hand the number of times I have gotten to sit under her teaching in person. Each time I was mesmerized, thoughts whirling, unable to write fast enough. Each time I was challenged, edified, and humbled. This book yielded the same result. *Alive in Him* is a precious chance to sit at Gloria's feet and hear Ephesians expounded with grace and clarity. Get your pen ready."

Jen Wilkin, author, *Women of the Word*; Bible study teacher

Alive in Him

Alive in Him

*How Being Embraced by the Love of
Christ Changes Everything*

Gloria Furman

Foreword by J. I. Packer

WHEATON, ILLINOIS

Alive in Him: How Being Embraced by the Love of Christ Changes Everything

Copyright © 2017 by Gloria C. Furman

Published by Crossway
        1300 Crescent Street
        Wheaton, Illinois 60187

Published in association with the literary agency of Wolgemuth & Associates, Inc.

Cover design: Josh Dennis

Cover image: Lettering by Four Hats Press

First printing 2017

Printed in the United States of America

Trade paperback ISBN: 978-1-4335-4977-9
ePub ISBN: 978-1-4335-4980-9
PDF ISBN: 978-1-4335-4978-6
Mobipocket ISBN: 978-1-4335-4979-3

Library of Congress Cataloging-in-Publication Data

Names: Furman, Gloria, 1980– author.
Title: Alive in him : how being embraced by the love of Christ changes everything / Gloria Furman ; foreword by J. I. Packer.
Description: Wheaton, Illinois : Crossway, [2017] | Includes bibliographical references and index.
Identifiers: LCCN 2016026236 (print) | LCCN 2016034395 (ebook) | ISBN 9781433549779 (tp) | ISBN 9781433549809 (ePub) | ISBN 9781433549786 (PDF) | ISBN 9781433549786 (pdf) | ISBN 9781433549793 (mobi) | ISBN 9781433549809 (epub)
Subjects: LCSH: Bible. Ephesians—Criticism, interpretation, etc.
Classification: LCC BS2695.52 .F86 2017 (print) | LCC BS2695.52 (ebook) | DDC 227/.507—dc23
LC record available at https://lccn.loc.gov/2016026236

Crossway is a publishing ministry of Good News Publishers.

LB		27	26	25	24	23	22	21	20	19	18	17
15	14	13	12	11	10	9	8	7	6	5	4	3	2	1

For the saints who dwell in these desert
lands and are faithful in Christ Jesus

Contents

Foreword

Out of the blue, by FedEx, came this manuscript, with cover letters from author and publisher, asking me to provide a foreword. The author's name was new to me, but I turned some pages and quickly found myself back in the days when, at the ripe old age of twenty-two, I stood before a class of war veterans, all older and no doubt wiser than me, to prepare them for a denominational exam on Ephesians in Greek, which they had to pass in order to proceed to the pastorate. (Full disclosure: they all made it, I am thankful to say.)

Whence this jolting of memory? Not from any similarity of teaching style. My job was textual, exegetical, and academic, and my way of doing it, as I recall, was phlegmatic and plodding, whereas Gloria Furman is exuberant, flamboyant, and topical, darting to and fro at high speed to make her points. Nor does any matching of resources come into it; I drew, I remember, mainly on Thomas Goodwin the Puritan and a High Church Anglican named Armitage Robinson, but there are no Puritans in Furman's reading list, and the Anglicans there are far from Robinson's type.

What then made my memory bell ring so loudly? It was the perception that digging into Ephesians had thrilled Mrs. Fur-

man's socks off, just as deep down it had done mine two generations ago (and, for the record, still does). Shared enthusiasm
was the trigger factor. Paul's concentrated layout in Ephesians
of the glory of God's grace—the life-giving, price-paying love
of the Father, the life-reshaping mediation of the Son, and the
life-transforming ministry of the Holy Spirit—is breathtaking;
Gloria Furman feels it, as do I, and evidently we agree that every
healthy Christian will feel the same, now and to all eternity.

There is a link of some kind between Ephesians and Colossians. Colossians is often viewed as Ephesians shrunk, but the
more natural guess is that Ephesians is Colossians enlarged and
generalized into a circular letter that Paul's aide-de-camp Tychi-
cus would take to a group of churches (see Eph. 6:21), leaving
a copy with each. Of this group Ephesus was the church that
Paul knew best, so it would not be strange if, when Paul's letters
were collected, this one would be tagged "To the Ephesians"
simply. But be that as it may be, what is certain is that Paul's
definitive declaration on church life is found here, just as his
definitive declaration on gospel life is found in Romans, with
the two together yielding his definitive teaching on Christian
life as such—life, that is, through, from, in, with, for, and under
the Lord Jesus Christ, the Son of God and Savior of sinners, the
really real Redeemer, risen, reigning, and returning, now and
henceforth forever, by the Father's appointment, Lord of all.

The whole of this comes into focus in Gloria Furman's applicatory overview of Ephesians, and of fellowship with Christ
according to Ephesians, which I enthusiastically commend as
vitamin-packed nourishment for Christians everywhere.

J. I. Packer

Preface

Do you read other people's mail? If you opened a letter that began, "To the saints who are in Ephesus and are faithful in Christ Jesus," you might not think the contents of that letter were for you. Unless, of course, you were a Turkish Christian reading the Bible on your balcony in Ephesus on a warm spring afternoon while you boiled finely ground coffee beans in a *cezve*!

Think of the book you are holding in your hands like one of those Lonely Planet guides that you can buy to prepare for travel abroad. The guidebook itself isn't the experience but something you read to whet your appetite for the real thing. It would be a sad state of affairs to only read about the views from the observation deck of the Burj Khalifa and leave it at that, thinking that you've felt the exhilarating dizziness of standing on the 126th floor of the world's tallest building, with the hot desert air blowing in your face. Paul's letter to the Ephesians is the real deal; my book is a mere bookmark.

Because Ephesians is God's Word, all of it is to be treasured, obeyed, shared, and meditated upon. God's Word is eternal. My little book on the themes of Ephesians is not eternal. If you want to know more about Ephesians but settle for just reading this book, then you will lose out. What you and I both need is to feed on God's Word; it's not a mere part of life, but it is our *very* life (Deut. 32:47). My goal is to lead you deeper into the text of the Bible so that you can see for yourself just how wide and long and high and deep is the mind-boggling love of Christ (Eph. 3:18–19). I really hope you'll read *Alive in Him* in the context of community. Because it's based on the text of the Bible, it is best to read, discuss, and apply what you're learning with other people. Plus all of the *you*'s in Ephesians are really plural *y'alls* or *youz guyz*!

These themes—the new humanity; Christ the head of all things; seated in heavenly places with Christ; a reordered cosmos; spiritual armor—all have the potential of sounding to rational ears like spiritual delusion or fantasy. To those who are tired of their sin and sick of the revolting evil in the world, what Paul has written sounds too good to be true. Is Jesus just our personal Peter Pan who takes us to Neverland, where we never have to face the facts of life? Is Ephesians describing an imaginary playground where Christians go on a farcical spiritual holiday while real wars rage back in the real world? Or is the picture of reality that we're given in Ephesians the true reality? And is it really as awe-full and terrifyingly beautiful as the letter says it is? Let's pray that God would give us eyes to see.

Acknowledgments

I am indebted to the men and women who have taught and are teaching me how to read the Bible. These saints spur me on to know what is the hope to which he has called us and have specially shaped the way I approach Paul's letter to the Ephesians: John Piper, Greg Beale, Kevin Vanhoozer, Tony Reinke, Graeme Goldsworthy, Michael Reeves, Elisabeth Elliot, and Timothy Gombis. Their influence is all over the pages of this book.

Ephesians reminds me to praise God for the faithful witness of two young women who winsomely pointed out to a fellow college student the fact of her spiritual deadness. I had no idea that I was dead in the trespasses and sins I was walking in, and when Tiffany James and Tiffany Sumlin shared the gospel with me in a freshman girls' Bible study, I was floored. I'm eternally grateful for these sisters in Christ who patiently explained to me that God is rich in mercy, and because of the great love with which he loved us (even when we were dead in our trespasses!) he made us alive together with Christ. Thank you, God, for the cross. By grace we have been saved!

I consider it one of the greatest privileges of my life to be a member of my local church, Redeemer Church of Dubai. Thank you for reveling in the mystery together with me—that we are members of the same body and partakers of the promise of Christ Jesus through the gospel. Every time we gather, it is a profound joy to display the manifold wisdom of God to the world and beyond and to catch a glimpse of the new creation, where people from every tribe and nation worship Jesus together.

Special thanks go to Robert Peterson, Andrew Wolgemuth, and Katlyn Griffin for using their various gifts to equip me to write this book. Thank you to Crossway for leveraging all their resources to spread God's Word to every corner of the globe. I'm so thankful for J. I. Packer's faithful ministry and books and for the generous foreword he contributed for *Alive in Him*. My life has been forever marked by Dr. Packer, particularly through his compelling book *Evangelism and the Sovereignty of God*, which taught me with no lack of enthusiasm that "we are all under orders to devote ourselves to spreading the good news, and to use all our ingenuity and enterprise to bring it to the notice of the whole world."[1]

A scholar has said that if you understand eschatology, you will undoubtedly enjoy your spouse all the more. (I think he could have been paraphrasing Ephesians.) To my dear husband, Dave, thank you for modeling the Christlike love described and commanded in Ephesians. Your determination to love me in the way that Christ loves his church points me to my Savior.

Thank you to the families and churches who enable us to serve. God uses your support and encouragement to help us put on the readiness given by the gospel of peace as shoes for our feet. We couldn't run with the gospel without you.

And to the sovereign God who made me alive together with Christ and saved me by grace, forever thanks and praise belong to you.

What Ephesians Is—and Isn't

Often when we read Ephesians we think of its content in lists: lists of the blessings we have in Christ; lists of who submits to whom in the household; lists of the pieces of our spiritual armor. The lists are there, but there are no bullet points in Ephesians. Instead of reading Ephesians to make lists, we should approach it expecting to see what is there in the context in which it is presented. In its most basic interpretation, the first half of Ephesians describes a narrative picture of what Jesus has accomplished through his cross; the second half of the letter describes how we can walk in the light of that reality.

Our expectations for our study of this letter should be high, and no doubt Ephesians will not disappoint. I haven't read a more effusive description of the letter than this one by pastor and theologian Martyn Lloyd-Jones:

> There are statements and passages in this Epistle which really baffle description. The great Apostle piles epithet upon epithet, adjective upon adjective, and still he cannot express

himself adequately. There are passages in [the] first chapter, and others in the third chapter, especially towards its end, where the Apostle is carried out above and beyond himself and loses and abandons himself in a great outburst of worship and praise and thanksgiving. I repeat, therefore, that there is nothing more sublime in the whole range of Scripture than this Epistle to the Ephesians.[1]

Nothing more sublime! Ephesians presents the sweeping panorama of history—from before the world began to after God re-creates all things at the end of this age. The stage was set in the mind of God since before time began, and the scenes move quickly. They even jump back and forth in time. Always, though, always running along is the almost slow-motion feeling of being swept up into the starry host to see the new heavens and the new earth being born. By grace we were chosen to participate in the drama. Could there be a greater privilege in all the universe?

Paul is describing the reordering of the cosmos in the person and work of Jesus Christ. Included in the macroscopic vision we see in Ephesians are detailed descriptions of Jesus's renewing and redeeming work. Essentially, we are given a picture of how he has reordered everything so that his will is done on earth as it is in heaven; we see what makes sense in this age now that he is the crucified, risen, ascended, and reigning cosmic Lord. Though we tarry, yet in this fallen world, his kingdom has come, is yet coming, and will imminently arrive in full. This age has been described in the timing of history as the "already but not yet" of Christ's kingdom, which is burgeoning full on the horizon. With faith-eyes enlightened by the Spirit, this is what should hold our heart's gaze when we read Ephesians.

Alive in Him is about what Ephesians is about. It is not a line-by-line commentary but a thematic treatment of the sublime truths in the letter. We have no need to "make Scripture come alive" when we read Ephesians, because Scripture is already alive (2 Tim. 3:16–17). Ephesians is not a dusty, doctrinal catalogue but a glorious vision pulsating with images of redeemed reality.

The riches of God's mercy to us in Christ Jesus are headline-making facts in the church. "You were predestined for adoption!" "You are the body of Christ!" "You were saved by grace through faith!" When we understand the implications of these realities, we experience the deepest peace and highest affections for God even though we remain in the body waiting for the Lord's return. There is a public-witness dimension to our new identity as well. The way we walk either personifics to the watching world what Christ is like (as we are *Christ*ians), or it shows a distortion of his image in us. Therefore, studying Ephesians and its content is not about making people aware of their blessings for the sake of self-esteem; it's about the glory of God our Father and the Lord Jesus Christ.

Ephesians describes in broad strokes and detailed lines how being embraced by the love of Christ changes *everything*. Because of Jesus there is a "new creation order" in effect from the highest echelon of the angelic order in heaven to the lowliest invertebrate growing in the deepest part of the deepest ocean. It is fitting that the Creator who made all things would redeem his creation. But what of the rebels, God's enemies who are loyal to the Devil and the world that is passing away? How can they be redeemed? God's glory is *the* answer. It is in beholding the glory of God in the face of Jesus Christ that we are changed.

That is a message we need to hear over and over again, especially in a world filled with counterfeit gospels that lead to our temporal disappointment and our eternal destruction. Since the Creator has created us with a capacity for hearing his Word, and he has spoken to us, our entire lives must be consumed with knowing and living his Word. While we tend to treat individual Bible verses like Band-Aids, Scripture testifies of itself that it is actually our very life (Deut. 32:47). The headlining banner over the individual Christian's life and the life of the church is that there is something more satisfying and more enduring than knowing that we are blessed. It is in knowing and being known by the triune God who is blessed forever. We learn about this God in his Word. Ephesians is a call to live according to that reality—walking in the knowledge of God in our daily lives with one another. As we run the race God has marked out before us, we look behind us to see that great cloud of witnesses of those who have finished their race. We also look to the ends of the earth to see our brothers and sisters who are also headed toward that Celestial City. We understand that our life is a vapor, and in understanding the frailty of our lives and the enduring truth of God, we pass down God's Word to the generations who will come after us. The path we trod is narrow, but it is not lonely! Ephesians calls us to walk faithfully with our eyes on eternity as it expands on the horizon and in our hearts.

Ephesians teaches us how to interpret the world around us according to eternal realities. Ephesians also takes us a step further into concrete application. We're shown how to walk in a manner worthy of the gospel we love as our doctrine is embodied in everyday life. I deeply appreciate how Kevin Vanhoozer summarizes the concept of Christian integrity:

> It's one thing to have a high view of Scripture; quite another to *do* its truth. It's not enough to admire the Bible; we have to embody it. Being biblical is not simply a matter of believ-

ing its propositions but of responding to the many things God is saying to us in Scripture. Because God *does* do more than convey information to us through the Bible, so those of us who read the Bible have to be more than information processors. A robust view of biblical authority requires us to obey its commands, trust promises, sing its songs, heed its wisdom, and hope for its ending.[2]

In the course of Ephesians we are given a distinctly Christian worldview that addresses the age-old problem of evil: why do God's children suffer pain and loss if Christ is on the throne? We are comforted regarding the reality of the unseen realm around us: should we be frightened of the powers and authorities if Christ is exalted far above them? The narrow vision we have for our lives is shown on the canvas of eternity. What are we to make of the mundane moments of our days? Do they matter in God's grand scheme of things? Ephesians reminds us how we have "learned Christ," and how his gospel utterly trans-forms literally everything. No realm is untouched—the life of the mind, our emotions, our families, our jobs, our prayers, our worries—everything is subject to the rule and sway of the will of Jesus. We cannot escape or outrun the future grace we have been given in Christ, and our daily lives are profusely marked by God's love and mercy.

A holy invasion to fill the void in our hearts has been in-augurated through the Spirit, who descends on believers and remains in them. Jesus has bound the strong man and plundered his house, and we are the captives he has released and leads in his train. Jesus is fearlessly and perfectly accomplishing the mis-sion of God to rescue and redeem his children in every corner of the globe. As C. S. Lewis would say, in his world-renowned Chronicles of Narnia, "Aslan is on the move."

1

Blessed in Christ

The Recipients of God's Rich Grace

EPHESIANS 1:1-14

In the cult classic film *Back to the Future*, teenager Marty McFly travels back in time and interacts with people in the 1950s. When Marty begins to understand the potential repercussions of his time travel exploits, he says that it's "heavy." His friend Doc, confused by the colloquial phrase from the future, asks, "Why are things so heavy in the future? Is there a problem with the earth's gravitational pull?" Doc is awestruck by the idea that something as fundamental to life as gravity could be an entirely different experience for people in the future. The irony in the script, of course, is that Doc is also thinking about something that is "heavy."

Whoa—This Is Heavy

There are many passages in the Bible that we tend to think of as too heavy to comprehend. And we would be right! The letter of Paul to the Ephesians is six short chapters, yet its content is loaded down with a weight of glory that boggles the mind and overwhelms the senses. Some people might pick up this heavy passage in the first chapter, skim over it, and walk away un- fazed. I've done this myself on occasion, my eyes glossing over the mega-sentence as my mind drifts to wondering what's for supper. But despite our mortal minds and the distractions that surround us on every side, we have every reason to be encour- aged as we labor to press into these truths. This is because the heaviness of this massive paragraph is really a weight of glory that we are meant to bear.

Ephesians is heavy, glorious truth—a burden that can be borne only on the back of humility. So it is with prayerful, hum- ble hearts that we open this book together.

Are We Reading Other People's Mail?

Paul opens his letter with a customary, customized introduc- tion. He says that he is "an apostle of Christ Jesus by the will of God." If his authority was initially ambiguous to any readers, let all doubts be washed away in this tsunami of commissioning. God himself, the creator and sustainer of the universe, the one who calls himself "I am," decreed that Paul is an apostle of his one and only Son, who has been given authority over all things. The words in this letter carry with them the authority of the one who sends the message. The sender is God. The words are God's Word. God is exalted in his power; who is a teacher like him? Can he be instructed? God says and does what he pleases; who can question him (Job 36:22–23; Rom. 11:34)?

God invented our human minds by which we peer into the words that have their origin in his mind. When we hold the Bible in our hands, we are holding a book of unfathomable significance and authority because it is God's Word. Our ability to acknowledge this fact is evidence of God's mercy in our lives. Our Creator does not owe us anything; it is benevolence of infinite kindness that God would speak to us and to do so in such a way that we might understand. Living wholeheartedly according to his Word, as we are well aware, requires a powerful work of grace that comes from the almighty God himself.

The phrase in 1:1 that describes the Ephesian Christians as "faithful in Christ Jesus" is startling. Is Paul using flattery to win over his readers by calling them "faithful"? Admittedly, I do this as a mother sometimes, but I like to think of it as something more positive such as vision casting. "Would my helpful children please come set the table for dinner?" I want to summon my youngsters to rise to the occasion and prove their helpfulness. Is Paul trying to cast a vision for the Ephesians to prove they are faithful? No, this is neither empty flattery nor inspiring vision casting. Paul is calling it like it is. If you are "in Christ Jesus," then by definition you are *faithful.* That's why this introduction is startling. If you looked back on the last day of your inner dialogue, spoken (or typed) words to others, emotional leanings, et cetera, you would have a hard time coming to the conclusion that you are the embodiment of godly faithfulness. So we must be reading someone else's mail, right? How does Paul get away with saying that we are faithful? Because we are "in Christ." This little term—*in Christ*—is actually the subject of a host of weighty ideas and expressions that are developed throughout the New Testament. Paul calls Christians those who are "in Christ." This in-ness is a one-ness: because Christ is alive forevermore, so we are alive in him. As you read Ephesians, keep an eye out for phrases such as "in Christ" and "in the Lord." Paul will spend the rest of his letter describing what life looks like as a result of being one with Christ—*in* Christ.

Becoming a Christian is a result of being in Christ. It is not merely our countenance, manners, religious habits, or other externalities that have changed since we were made alive in him. At the moment of our conversion we were altered at the very core of our being. The life of Christ is now in us. Anglican theologian Richard Sibbes put it like this:

> Before those opposed to each other can be friends, there must be an alteration; and this alteration must be either on God's part, or on ours. . . . On a musical instrument, those strings that are out of tune are adjusted to those that are in tune. In the same way, it is we who must alter, and not God.[1]

Once we were God's enemies; we are now reconciled to him through his Son. And it is in his Son where we will remain forever. Paul doesn't call us "saints" because we are holy people in and of ourselves. He doesn't call us saints because a religious organization has conferred on us the title. He calls us saints because God has set us apart and placed us in his Son. Our "saintliness" is because of what Christ has done on our behalf. We belong to God as his holy people by his own initiative and Christ's work on the cross. Ours is to respond in faith to this gospel. Paul's introductory blessing is apropos, a statement of fact that we mustn't allow our hearts to miss the thrill of pondering. "Grace to you and peace from God our Father and the Lord Jesus Christ" (Eph. 1:2).

The Fulfillment of the Sanguine Psalm 103

The blessings we have in Christ are more than social niceties like saying "Gesundheit" after someone sneezes. Paul is describing how we have been blessed "with every spiritual blessing." Often, when we hear of these blessings, we just smile and nod and utter a polite "Thanks," as though someone has just blessed a sneezing fit. "Spiritual blessings" sounds fake, like a warranty for an appliance that expires the moment you open the package and use the machine. That warranty was never meant to benefit you, the consumer. But God's blessings are utterly real. The indwelling Holy Spirit is the one who mediates these blessings to us; he brings them to us and applies them to our lives. In this section Paul writes to unwrap these blessings in a massive sentence that spreads from verses 3–14 in the original Greek (202 words!).

This lengthy sentence at first seems like a flourish of random ideas, but Paul is actually quite intentional. Have you ever noticed that in all the other major world religions it is polite and common to ask for "God's" blessings or to say, "Praise God"? Notice in this passage how Paul moves through each person of the Holy Trinity and repeats certain phrases. He notes that God is the Father of our Lord Jesus Christ, a notation that highlights this as a *distinctly Christian* composition of praise to God.

This opening passage in Ephesians echoes Psalm 103, where God calls us to trust him as we walk in this fallen world. This psalm anticipates what we have been given through Christ, which is "every spiritual blessing in the heavenly places" (Eph. 1:3). Bless the Lord, oh my soul! Don't forget a single one of these blessings! These blessings find their origin in him, and their bestowment upon us is entirely of God's own initiative. It is he who blessed us, chose us, predestined us, lavished his grace on us, made known his purposes to us, and accomplishes all these things for us. All this he has done "to the praise of his glorious grace, with which he has blessed us in the Beloved"

(Eph. 1:6). The blessings of Psalm 103, which are specifically fulfilled through Jesus and described in Ephesians 1:3–14, are both wrought of God's glory in his Son and bestowed through the gleaming mercy shown to us at the cross. God's saving purposes are from eternity past in the council of the Trinity, and "in all wisdom and insight" (v. 8) he lavishes his grace on all those he chooses.

A Gift for You

In my experience in sharing the gospel, I've noticed that most people do not contend with the idea that God is mighty to save and that he indeed retains the prerogative to save sinners (because he is, after all, *God*). What most people do take issue with is his willingness to save them and change them. "Sure, right. I know he can save me. *But would he?*" God's willingness is called into question, and his willingness is usually evaluated from the vantage point of that person's fluctuating, circumstantially based emotions. If you struggle with this (I'm raising my hand here too), then watch how the record gets set straight in verses 4–6. It says that we were chosen before the foundation of the world. This is no last-minute grab off the shelf when you reach the cash register.

Our salvation is not the effect of a thoughtless impulse buy, but it is the impulse of the holy, triune God who determined to save us from before the foundation of the world. He chose us not because we were already holy and blameless like he is (we weren't). Perhaps hearing that your being chosen is not because of your goodness is news to you. You may have been under the impression that God owed it to you to save you because you worked so hard to please him. Many of us may even balk at such an understanding of salvation and think, *I would never believe that! I know that salvation is all about grace.* Even so, we may still be tempted to live as though God were obligated to bless us because of our goodness. I become aware of this struggle in my own heart any time I suffer a trial and wonder, "Why me?"

Remembering that God chose us to be holy and blameless before him rather than because we were already holy and blameless is a freedom bell in the sinner's heart. We're comforted by this doctrine when we're feeling sheepish and vulnerable. God chose us. Let gospel freedom ring!

The Guiding Thermostat in Paul's Letter

The oven in our apartment is a mystery to me. The markings on the dials have long been worn off by previous tenants. When the workers come to replace the empty gas tank for the oven, I excuse myself to the living room (as is appropriate culturally). If I bake cupcakes, they might lean to the left or the right indiscriminately. At Thanksgiving time the only sure bet for roasting the turkey properly is a trusty meat thermometer and lots of patience, and an adventurous spirit. I have so many questions about my oven that may never be answered, but I do have tools that can help me begin to understand how to avoid burning pancakes (too badly).

The mysterious passages in Ephesians are like that oven. We tend to examine Ephesians in disjointed sections and walk away with questions such as:

- How do you put on the seemingly out-of-place spiritual armor in chapter 6 (and why)?
- What does a modern man or woman do with the "household code" in chapter 5?
- How can sinners live out the call to holiness in chapter 4?

- Is it possible to see the unity of God's people in chapter 3 even amid our hundreds of denominations?
- How do we live out the ramifications of salvation by grace in chapter 2?
- And who can wrap their mind around the spiritual blessings in chapter 1?

When these issues are considered in isolation, they tend to take on an air of frustrating futility. The cupcakes will always turn out lopsided no matter what I do, so why bother? While this might be an understandable sentiment, don't give up on the cupcakes! They're worth every bit of effort you put into discovering how to see them turn out right-side up. There *is* a guiding thermostat, if you will, in Ephesians. (Please forgive my return to the dessert illustration—I have an incurable sweet tooth.) The overarching message of Ephesians, the fountain from which every doctrinal truth emerges is Ephesians 1:9–10:

> . . . making known to us the mystery of his will, according to his purpose, which he set forth in Christ as a plan for the fullness of time, to unite all things in him, things in heaven and things on earth.

Let Earth Receive Her King

God is blessed for revealing his mysterious plan from eternity past and bringing it to fruition in eternity future. When we struggle with the question of our purpose and of the purpose of the world, Ephesians 1:9–10 gives us God's comprehensive answer. God is glorified through his "making known to us the mystery of his will, according to his purpose, which he set forth in Christ as a plan for the fullness of time, to unite all things in him, things in heaven and things on earth."

When God created Adam and Eve, he blessed them. Then he

charged them with the privilege of stewardship over his creation. "Be fruitful and multiply and fill the earth and subdue it, and have dominion over the fish of the sea and over the birds of the heavens and over every living thing that moves on the earth" (Gen. 1:28). Men and women were to rule justly and mercifully under God's authority, leading and nurturing all he put in their care. But mankind rejected God's authority through their sin, and as a result the creation became subjected to futility.

Take a two-second glance at the news headlines for today and you will observe that mankind fails to rule creation with justice and mercy. But the Bible is God's story of redemption. There will be a Son of Man ruling from the throne. Jesus said to his disciples, "Truly, I say to you, in the new world, when the Son of Man will sit on his glorious throne, you who have followed me will also sit on twelve thrones, judging the twelve tribes of Israel" (Matt. 19:28; see also Rev. 3:21). Jesus is the one who rules unequivocally over everything in heaven and on earth. We read in Ephesians 1:9–10 the end goal of all things, the all-encompassing reason for everything that ever was or will be—the *anakephalaiōsis*. That is a deeply profound term that means "summing up." Although we are only a mere ten verses into Ephesians, this statement is the climax of the entire epistle. Ephesians shows us how Jesus, the Son of Man, has come to his throne. The rest of this letter draws out the implications of Christ's enthronement. There are implications not only for us as individuals who love the Lord and long for his return when every knee bows to him and every tongue confesses he is Lord, but also for us collectively as members of Christ's body, the church.

One of those implications is that the summing up of all things in Christ summons forth our authenticity. The world is all kinds of crazy (again, just skim the newspaper headlines), but a life lived in light of this doctrine is coherent. When we reject or ignore the mystery God has made known (Christ as the focal point of all things), we are out of step with God's purposes for the cosmos. Centered on ourselves, we are cosmic renegades. Centered on Christ, we are utterly authentic in the most genuine sense of the word. The relevancy of the *anakephalaiōsis* to our daily lives (both now and tomorrow and in eternity) is the consistency (or congruence or uniformity or correspondence) of our lives with ultimate reality. It also motivates us to carry the gospel to people groups who have not yet heard of Christ and who are perishing for this lack of knowledge.

This consistency of our lives in accordance with this truth is no mere rote submission but rather adoring love with corresponding speech overflowing from *hearts* filled to overflowing with sincere fealty and love for Christ our head. It is sober *minds* that think thoughts that are in line with God's truth and are confident in the sufficiency, authority, and clarity of his Word. It is *doing* all things as service rendered unto the Lord by his strength that God supplies for Christ's glory—that he might be glorified in all things. A Monday morning at the office lived in line with the summing up of all things in Christ is a depiction of utter authenticity. The resolution of a conflict over even the dumbest of things (as many conflicts often are), when done in accordance with the supremacy of Christ, is evidence of Christ's loving rule. We are doomed to live a confusing and false existence as long as we live in denial of the universal headship of Jesus. But when we humbly repent of the notion that we can live independently from God and instead cling to Jesus, then we walk in truth.

We'll explore more implications of this later on in the chapter and throughout the book. For now, I want to discuss a few key phrases in the mega-sentence of verses 3–14.

What Is Predestination?

First, we'll come to the oft-misunderstood term *predestination*. It ought to be mentioned that predestination is not about God collecting humans because he thinks they make nice robots to fill his heavenly warehouses. Far from it! The biblical picture of predestination describes the intentions of a loving Father who predestined us for adoption as sons because he wanted to ("according to the purpose of his will") so that his grace would be enjoyed and magnified. Jesus said, "In my Father's house are many rooms. If it were not so, would I have told you that I go to prepare a place for you?" (John 14:2). This is the picture of genuine adoption of full sons and daughters, not the collecting of robots for manipulation.

The "p-word" also raises other questions—thoughtful questions about those who are not chosen, unreached people groups, unborn children, and many other heart-stirring questions. One thing that we can assuredly affirm across the board (no matter where you land in the complexity of things regarding predestination) is that God is God. God is the one in charge, and he has chosen to save us to this tune—"to the praise of his glorious grace" (Eph. 1:6). Whereas in the Old Testament God chose Israel to be a people holy to the Lord out of all the peoples who are on the face of the earth, it was not for any reason other than the one God himself gave. He chose them because he set his love on them (Deut. 7:6–8). And now, as it says in this passage in Ephesians, God chooses to set his affection on us—those who are in Christ—personally, individually, and irrevocably.

Our chosenness is what sets us apart, and our being in

Christ is what enables us to walk in his ways. The church, as Peter explains, is "a chosen race, a royal priesthood, a holy nation, a people for his own possession." And all of this so that we may "proclaim the excellencies of him who called you out of darkness into his marvelous light" (1 Pet. 2:9). The church is the embodiment of God's new creation on earth, ever-increasing and expanding to fill the earth with the knowledge of the Lord by making disciples of all nations, obeying God's creation mandate and his Son's Great Commission. Who is sufficient for these things? God has done all this for the sake of the Beloved, his Son, whom he loves. All praise belongs to the God who is both able and willing to save.

When Jesus Cleans House

What does it mean to be "sealed by the Holy Spirit?" Have you ever wondered why Jesus told his disciples before he ascended that it would be better for them if he went away? This passage really puzzled me as a new believer. In the years since then, I've grown to appreciate and better understand the doctrine of the indwelling Spirit of God. The reason Jesus says this is that he (together with the Father) is going to send the Holy Spirit to live *in* his followers. He is the blessing by which we receive all the spiritual blessings Ephesians 1 is talking about.

In his Farewell Discourse before he ascended back into heaven, Jesus blessed his disciples and promised that he will send another *Paraclete* (John 14:16). This benediction before his ascension was surprising, though, given the fact of his imminent departure. But his ascension actually provides the avenue by which we are able to be connected forever to the ascended Christ. When he returns to heaven, Jesus sends his

Spirit, who descends upon and dwells in all his disciples in every place. Paul says in 1:13–14 that we "were sealed with the promised Holy Spirit, who is the guarantee of our inheritance until we acquire possession of it, to the praise of his glory."

When you were growing up, your mom may have encouraged you to clean your room, saying, "Cleanliness is next to godliness." In the time since, you may have learned the axiom that literal, physical cleanliness—like dust-free baseboards and mildew-less grout—is *not* a credit to your personal holiness. For example, it is possible for a housewife to clean her house so perfectly that guests could eat off the floor although she is a desperately depraved housewife who is far from God.

It is soul-liberating news that unsoiled bathroom floors are not a requirement for fellowship with a holy God. Yet in a very real sense, *spiritual* cleanliness *is* godliness. I began to appreciate aspects of that particular kind of cleanliness when reflecting on the testimonies of believers in Christ who had been previously influenced or possessed by unclean spirits. Dead in their trespasses and submitted to the wills of unclean spirits, these men and women behaved in accordance with the unclean, ungodly character of the spirit that occupied their "house."

What does this anecdote have to do with believers being "sealed with the promised Holy Spirit?" If you spoke to these men and women, you would hear them testify to the lordship of Christ over every dark power as he "cleaned house" and sent the Spirit of truth to indwell them and seal them forever. Indeed, whether we have a similar testimony or not, *all* those who are not in the flesh but in the Spirit ought to praise the Father and the Son for sending the Spirit.

The Holy Spirit can never be served an eviction notice. Not ever. Contrary to unclean spirits, the Holy Spirit's fruit is *godly*: love, joy, peace, patience, kindness, goodness, faithfulness, and self-control (Gal. 5:22–23). That's why Christians are instructed to "walk by the Spirit, and you will not gratify the desires of the flesh" (Gal. 5:16), and not to "grieve" (Eph. 4:30) or "quench" (1 Thess. 5:19) the Spirit. The presence of the indwelling, sealing Spirit is a testament to God's comprehensive, unmitigated ownership over us; he doesn't merely pay rent. "Or do you not know that your body is a temple of the Holy Spirit within you, whom you have from God? You are not your own, for you were bought with a price. So glorify God in your body" (1 Cor. 6:19–20). What a thrill and a wonder it is to have been given God's Spirit! And what an assurance and assurer he is of God's love as he occupies our hearts.

In his book *Of the Mortification of Sin in Believers*, John Owen said this of the Spirit's dwelling in our hearts and the consequential yearning for holiness that he produces in us:

> Among those who walk with God, there is no greater motive and incentive unto universal holiness, and the preserving of their hearts and spirits in all purity and cleanness than this: That the blessed Spirit, who has undertaken to dwell in them, is continually considering what they give entertainment in their hearts unto, and rejoices when his temple is kept undefiled.[2]

The Spirit is repulsed by something that is more despicable than filth and more deadly than rogue germs; he hates sin. Cleansed by the blood of the Son and enabled by the Spirit, who desires to please the Father in everything, we can make war against our sin and put to death the deeds of the flesh. We'll discuss this more as we continue our reading in Ephesians.

And That's Not All!

Our heavenly Father has set aside a place for us in his new heaven and new earth, which is an inheritance unlike any this world has ever seen. For a description of this inheritance see Revelation 21:1–22:5.[3] Dual realities are in play here: we have both obtained our inheritance (1:11) and wait to acquire it (1:14). The new heaven and the new earth are ours through Christ. The evidence of this is that we have been sealed in the resurrected Christ by means of the Spirit. Our participation in resurrection began when we were born again. "That is, the Spirit himself is viewed as the very beginning of this inheritance and not just a guarantee of the promise of its coming. The Spirit, who would be present fully throughout the future new cosmos, has entered in part into believers, so that they have begun to obtain the inheritance of the new earth."[4]

And through Jesus, who accomplished for us a "new exodus" out of our slavery to sin, we have become *God's* inheritance. "But the LORD has taken you and brought you out of the iron furnace, out of Egypt, to be a people of his own inheritance, as you are this day" (Deut. 4:20).

We are his inheritance, we have obtained an inheritance, and we are yet waiting for our inheritance. The dynamic of this "already–not yet" is manifest in our lives every day. "Paul's emphasis on God's past act of raising Christ from the dead and exalting him at his right hand in the heavenly places reveals the emphasis in Ephesians on the eschatological 'already.'"[5] We have already been given the Spirit and have been adopted, *and* we who have "the firstfruits of the Spirit, groan inwardly as we wait eagerly for adoption as sons, the redemption of our bodies" (Rom. 8:23). And so we are "sorrowful, yet always rejoicing; as poor, yet making many rich; as having nothing, yet possessing everything" (2 Cor. 6:10). We are given strength of heart to acknowledge the truth of the depravity of the world we live in, but we grieve with hope (1 Thess. 4:13). Being indwelt by the Holy Spirit "on this side of eternity" is not the end of the story for us. God has "put his seal on us and given us his Spirit in our hearts as a guarantee" (2 Cor. 1:22). The gift of the indwelling Spirit is a foretaste of what is to come.

We do not yet possess our inheritance, but the presence of the Spirit in us is a guarantee from God that we will surely possess it. There is no greater assurance we could have. Though we live in this broken and fragmented cosmos, we see with faith-eyes that in the fullness of time there will be a day in which all things will be united under the sovereign rule of Christ (Eph. 1:9–10).

Reminded of Whose We Are

Ephesians reminds us of reality. We are in Christ and we have been given the mind of Christ. Using the mind of Christ, we imagine ways that we might more fully enjoy Jesus and invite others to do the same.

I think that one of the best ways I have been reminded of this fact recently is through the cheerful antics of my young children, who constantly seek my attention so that I can share in their joy. "Look at me, Mommy! I'm a flying super guy," my preschool-aged son cries out as he leaps off of furniture. My quiet artist brings me pictures she has drawn, and she lingers at my side, watching my face as I behold what she has created. I ask her, "Will you tell me about this right here?" as I point out a detail in her work. She erupts into giggles, and a stream of glee comes out as she describes what she has drawn with flourish. Even as babies they are on to the secret of fulfilling the joy of others. As my youngest was learning to walk, he would squawk like a parrot until he was certain that he had my undivided attention as he held onto the bedside with one arm, waving the other like a wing getting ready for takeoff. My oldest child writes me letters filled with whimsy that she knows will make me smile. We were made to live in such a way that our deepest joy is found in seeking the joy of others. When the light of the gospel shines in our hearts, it is clear as day that the joy we are seeking is found in Christ, and we long to spend our lives introducing this joy to others, thus increasing our own joy in him evermore. Fueled by the love of Christ, our joy-seeking is purified and ever-expanding.

Understanding that being "in Christ" is our primary location, we live out who we are *in him*. Being embraced by the love of Christ changes everything as he transforms the way we live out the callings he has given us. How does being in Christ transform the way we do our jobs, the way we relate to other drivers on the road, the way we buy groceries, the way we speak to children, the way we think about growing older, and the way we steward our God-given talents? The immortality of Jesus and his indomitable power toward those he loves means that we have at our disposal every spiritual blessing in order to do his will for the fame of his name in all the earth.

Through Christ's power, we can live "to the praise of God's glory." The blessings we have been given in Christ are not carrots being dangled in front of us to reward our potential faithfulness; they are true gifts. Already ours in Christ! Because Jesus is the risen and ascended one who has sent us his Spirit, we don't have to hope that we will one day be given these gifts. God has graciously given us these transforming gifts to have and to live by faith, believing that they are ours in Christ. We have no need to live irrationally anymore, in ways that contradict the fact that we have these blessings in Christ. Through Christ's power we can live consistently according to *whose* we are.

Reminded of Our Mission

Who wants to embody the image of created things when we have been captivated by the love of Christ and empowered by his Spirit to be ministers of reconciliation? The mercy of God is currently being extended to everyone. The new humanity in Christ, recipients of God's rich mercy, is designed to be outward focused in extending God's mercy to the lost. But many of us regret that this missional lifestyle of invitation is a fleeting pursuit at times. We have those occasional "aha" moments when we remember the joy of our salvation and cannot help but be inclined to invite others to share in that joy. How many times have I proverbially kicked myself for being so self-centered that I've missed open doors to witness to the grace and mercy of Jesus on the cross to nonbelievers in my life? Being embraced by the love of Christ, and leaning in to the design God has for me as his ambassador, reframes the way I think about myself in relation to others.

As a member of the church, I remember that I have been given the ministry of reconciliation as God's ambassador to the nations. I'm part of the new humanity who blesses this cursed world. We lay down our artillery and lead the charge to use our God-given talents to build up others. We call off all social embargoes and step into diverse relationships in order that we may share the grace God has provided. We tear down our silos of personal and communal isolation to make room for the ever-expanding throng of festal revelers who are entering the kingdom of God. You can't bar the doors when you're waving a palm branch.

The Father is shaping me into the cruciform image of his

Son. Being reminded of this through these passages in Ephesians shows me that this is the primary reality in which I am living, and the reality into which I am inviting others. We have many more things to discuss regarding this particular implication of being "in Christ." We will do so in later chapters that deal specifically with community and the church.

Reminded to Live Authentically

The escapades that I imagine in my mind, where everyone stops what they are doing to spend energy adoring me, are a farce. There is no other god besides the Lord God. All pretenders are really just dumb and mute idols. This means that the idealized version of myself that I carry around in my heart—the me who everyone fawns over—is really just a shell of a human being drunk on the praise of man. All my plotting to this end is in vain. Even when I succeed at some level and earn some recognition that I've been working for (or get lucky and "the gods smile upon me"), I know in my heart that it's all just rubbish. It doesn't make me as happy as I can possibly be, and the buzz of the accolades certainly doesn't last as long as I want it to. The depth and quality of this kind of happiness is always found wanting. But having the mind of Christ reminds you that there is nothing greater than Jesus. The Holy Spirit will not allow you to live satisfied on the rubbish heap; he will nurture a longing for the City of God to beat in your heart.

When we imagine what it means to "live fully as God created you to be," this often comes with a host of earthly identities. We think of ourselves as embodying a kind of earthly role or brand. *"I'm going to have the smartest children at this school, and their success is going to bring me the admiration I desire." "I'm going to build the most enviable portfolio in my group of friends and*

41

they are going to seek out my opinions." "My body is going to look just like hers, and I'm going to enjoy all the benefits that come along with it." "My house is going to be the sanctuary of all sanctuaries, and it is going to give me the peace that I crave." "My dining table and stomach are going to be filled with this kind of food, and then I'll be able to look at myself in the mirror and be proud." The identity issue transcends stage of life, culture, gender, and economics. Not a single one of us is immune to the messages the world would like us to believe about ourselves. Messages are everywhere—we receive rapid-fire messages via television commercials, advertisements on social media, viral videos, and the like. We also actively *look for* things to attach to ourselves that bring us meaning and identity.

The world invites us to embody its image, buying and selling the lie that if you eat the fruit of knowledge apart from God, deciding what is good and evil, you will be gods. But our consciences, on which God has written eternity, know better. Hence the snide sarcasm of movements that scorn overt brands, ironically becoming earthly brands in themselves. Reflecting the glory of the world is not glorious; it is a slavish hell.

These truths in Ephesians remind us that we have been co-crucified and co-risen together with Christ, and we are to live accordingly, with our affections following suit. Jesus is the one who is worthy of all praise, and he is exalted above all. The only way that we can feel the rush of a life well-lived and rest easy in our soul is by living to revel in and reflect his image.

The Narrative That Eats All Other Narratives for Lunch

The life we long for is not the self-seeking life that the world in its perverse drama seeks to suck us into. The Christian faith offers the one authentic reality. In all our talk about competing stories—my story, your story, find your story, et cetera—we need biblical truth to clear the stage. Justin Taylor pointed out Michael Horton's helpful explanation of the one reality: the "counterdrama to all of the meganarratives and metanarratives of this passing age."[6] The life we long for is actually the one that gladly raises its glass at every occasion of weeping, laughing, working, defending, building, submitting, leading, serving, marrying, eating, and dying to humbly affirm that all things are "to the praise of *his* glory."

2

Called to Hope

A Prayer to Know Christ's
Power and Supremacy

EPHESIANS 1:15-23

This is the real deal. God has really done all these things for you. And he really will fulfill his promises to you. This is something that you're going to need to remember. You'll need to know this in a way that goes deeper than, "Yeah, I know that story." You'll need to know this in a working-knowledge kind of way that says, "I *live* this story." The story that Paul is spelling out in this letter includes the roles we all play. But more than merely learning lines to recite at the school play to get credit for your arts class, you need to have working knowledge of the plotline so that you can follow the lead of an unseen director and respond appropriately to the other actors around you. Welcome to Improv 101.[1]

Improv is not a free-for-all where actors may do whatever they please. Improv discerns what is already at play and follows along with creatively faithful interactions. The Christian life could be likened unto an improv. We're no mere robots; we are imagers who do our Father's will. We could say in this metaphor that the Father is our Director (and Executive Producer). He has given us his Word and his Spirit. We follow our Lead, his Son, who abides by the Script perfectly. Jesus sees what his Father is doing and imitates him, and we follow Jesus and do as he has told us to do. Even more, Jesus is working *through* us, his Spirit-empowered body.

As improv is not willy-nilly, neither is the Christian life. Michael Scott, the hapless manager in an American sitcom called *The Office*, was asked how he joined his improv class (his favorite hobby). He improv'ed a fantastical story, and then he honestly replied, embarrassed by the comparatively boring truth: "The real way was that I found a flyer."

We all come from different places, but the Lord has called each of us into his grand story through the same means: by grace through faith in Jesus Christ. Perhaps you feel as though you just stumbled your way into the Christian faith—as unintentionally as coming across a random flyer. Many Christians cannot remember a time when they were not Christians. Others of us know the exact date and time in which we were born again. I've heard some believers retell their salvation testimony with a twinge of embarrassment, kind of like Michael Scott did when asked about his improv class. "Oh, it was nothing special. Kind of a boring story, actually." I am always excited to remind brothers and sisters of this profound truth: there is no such thing as a boring "born-again birth story." If you have been redeemed out of the kingdom of darkness and transferred to the kingdom of God's Son, then your salvation was planned before time in the council of the triune Godhead. Any rescue that required the blood of the perfect Lamb of God and was planned by the Trinity could never be a boring rescue.

One other thing: observant readers will notice that Paul has commended the believers for their love toward "all" the saints (Eph. 1:15). There was no partiality in their love. No racism. No prejudice. No moral superiority toward any one. Both Jewish and Gentile Christians are together as one. Their faith is directed toward the one Lord Jesus Christ. Continue to look for the unification of these two spheres (Jews and Gentiles) throughout the rest of the letter. Over and over again you will see Paul highlight this beautiful and shocking implication of the gospel.

Wake Up and Smell the New Creation

Paul was not describing a new idea or philosophy for his readers to consider. He was proclaiming a new age. The crux of human history (the cross) is in the past, and the future is forever changed to fit in line with what Jesus accomplished on the cross. Adam's sons and daughters, the prisoners of sin and death, are freed through the sacrificial death of the last Adam. This "intrusion of a new world aeon" (or age) is the predominant theme in Paul's ministry.[2] Everything we apprehend about ourselves and the world around us must be interpreted in light of the one, permanent, all-encompassing reality: Jesus is infallibly putting the cosmos back together. The implications of this fact are legion, and the results can be seen only through eyes of faith.

God has already blessed us in Christ with every spiritual blessing. Praise God! And now Paul's prayer is simply that we might have our eyes opened to the implications of our new reality of having been blessed in Christ. Our praise to God and our prayer for more insight into his blessings belong together.

But these are no simple implications. How much do we really know of God's call, inheritance, and power? Since these things are ours through Christ, and Christ himself paid the highest price that we might have them, and Paul prayed that we would know these things, it seems critical that we might learn more of these things. If a rich uncle passes away and leaves behind his riches, how quickly would you run to the bank holding the letter from his attorney? Would you then linger outside the bank holding a closed account statement? Wouldn't you want to step boldly into the bank, inform the clerk of your presence, and listen eagerly with rapt attention to hear the news containing exactly what you've inherited?

In Christ Now and Thirty Trillion Years from Now

Paul's prayer is in light of all that God has done for us in Jesus (Eph. 1:1–14): "in Christ," "in him, "in the Beloved." What does it mean that we are "in Christ"?

Being "in Christ" is the overarching reality in which the people of God find themselves. It is like the key that interprets the map. The pan-ethnic bride of Christ is created by God to be a new humanity of people who are co-crucified, co-buried, and co-risen with Christ. God has placed us in Christ fully. No believer is half in or partly in Christ, but completely in Christ. If you have been crucified with Christ, then you have been permanently changed forever. This supernatural change is so drastic that you "no longer live." Of course, you are still *you*, but you are you *in Christ*. When Jesus died on the cross physically, your old self, who was a slave to sin, spiritually died. The chains of sin and the cords of death are broken.

When Paul says that we are "in Christ," he is applying that Old Testament principle or fact that we are represented by someone. That is, just as all Adam's offspring are "in" Adam, and just as the nation of Israel was represented by the priest who offered sacrifices or the king who led the people, so all believers are now in Christ.

When we see Paul using the phrase "in Christ," he is not merely saying that we are to walk in Christ's footsteps, as though the message of Christianity is merely that Christ followers do what Christ would do. We certainly ought to look like our Savior, but our moral performance is not the source of our justification. Christ's moral performance is the source of our justification, and being in Christ is being united to him and receiving all the blessings that are part of Christ in the heavenly places. Being "in Christ" is indeed the one great, permanent circumstance. If you are in Christ today, then thirty trillion years from now you will still be in Christ.

Seeing with the Eyes of the Heart

It is indisputable that we have a need for knowledge. We need light. In order to walk wisely in this world, we need to know the truth. My family lives downtown in an apartment building that was built on top of a shopping center. There are many eateries in this shopping center, most of which are really good. Some are exceptional, and only a few are downright undesirable.

One morning on our way to school we drove by one of the undesirable eateries, as usual. But this time as we drove by, my children gasped. The front of the restaurant was all boarded up.

This was a good sign, I said, because perhaps behind the boards they were tearing down the eatery to make way for something new and better. But alas, looks can be deceiving. "Oh no, Mom," my oldest child said. "There's a sign that says, 'Renovation in progress. We'll be back.'" What looked like a delightful scenario was actually a sign that the undesirable eatery was here to stay. And true to form, they renovated the inside of the restaurant, but the menu stayed the same.

God created humanity with a need for knowledge, and he ordained that we would live by the knowledge that is best for us, that is, the knowledge of him. He gave Adam and Eve his words, and they lived by every word that came from his mouth. The man and the woman lived in unbroken community with each other and with God until they took matters into their own hands. Literally.

At the Serpent's prompting, Eve considered the Tree of the Knowledge of Good and Evil. She saw that the tree God had forbidden was good for food, and the fruit was a delight to her eyes, and it would make her wise. Rejecting a life of living by God's words, she took the fruit of the tree and ate it (Gen. 3:6). Then she handed it to her husband, who was next to her. She was deluded with the Serpent's "plausible argument" (Col. 2:4) and taken captive by Satan's "empty deceit" (Col. 2:8). Eve seized the opportunity to obtain knowledge in a manner forbidden by God, even though she was created to functionally image God by knowing him and his will. Adam also failed to acknowledge God's will and walk in obedience to it, following his wife into sin. And all Adam's descendants would be born into the same spiritual blindness. And now we need the eyes of our hearts to be enlightened. We are the people who walk in darkness with a need to see the great light.

That's why Paul prayed this prayer for us. If the vision of our heart-eyes is nearsighted with narcissism or clouded with cataracts of pride, we're going to miss out on what God wants us to know. Paul prayed that the Spirit would make us wise to who God is and enlighten the eyes of our hearts (Eph. 1:17–18). This is in accordance with the way that God wants us to obtain knowledge. Satan's seeds of deception were reaped by Adam and Eve, and they gained knowledge by means of forbidden fruit. But Jesus gives us the Spirit, who opens our eyes to an increasing knowledge of God so that we bear fruit in every good work (Col. 1:9–10).

Paul prayed that the Holy Spirit might give us wisdom and revelation so that we would better understand God's plan and live accordingly. The Father of glory has revealed his mystery—his plan to unite all things in Christ. So here Paul prays that our eyes would be opened to this previously undisclosed reality. God will illumine our minds by his Spirit to grasp his revelation. Left to ourselves, we invent ridiculous things that serve to glorify ourselves only. We need the Spirit to open our eyes to God's truth, warm our hearts to love that truth, and empower us to live in line with the truth that God alone is worthy to be praised.

Let us, then, with the humble gratitude that ought to mark unworthy sinners, seek to see with the eyes of our heart the reality of God's purposes to give his children grace and glory. This reality that Ephesians speaks of is so certain that we can bank our lives on it. Those who are in Christ cannot help but see the reality that Christ has inaugurated. What's at stake is the difference between theory and experience. Paul's prayer for us is essentially that we would see reality and live in accordance with it.

Paul's Prayer

In Ephesians 1:15–23 Paul prays we would know more of God, specifically these three things:

1. God's call (hope)
2. God's inheritance (riches of glory)
3. God's power (immeasurable greatness)

This is astonishing to our modern sensibilities, because we have heard from our youth to know *ourselves*. Confused about your calling in life? Find out what you want, don't give up hope, and go get it. Sad that you don't have what you want? Work hard to achieve riches and glory. Frustrated that you are weak? Look inside you and see how immeasurably great you really are.

But Paul wants us to know more of *God*. God is the one who called us to a specific hope, promised us a future, and has the power to make it all come to pass just as he said. As Christians we are to re-mind ourselves with the mind of Christ (see 1 Cor. 2:16), looking to the character and promises of God. Since we are regenerate in Christ, our minds can now apprehend a correct understanding of who God is and what he is doing. We can see the world for what it really is and make decisions in line with God's revealed will. This is radically different from the world's encouragement to dig deeper inside yourself for understanding! God is the one who tells us what he has called us to, gives us the future that will satisfy us, and carries us all the way home.

These three things serve as an outline for Paul's prayer and form the body of what believers ought to think about their past, present, and future. No sphere or season of life is left untouched in this all-encompassing prayer.

Let's look at the first thing Paul says we need to know about God.

God's Call to Hope

We need to know God's call to hope. Remember that you came because he called you first. What is the hope he called you to? We need to know this so we don't live *functionally aimless*.

What kind of hope do we have? We are called to holiness—to be saints. We're loved by God and called to be saints (Rom. 1:7). This call to holiness is a community project because we're "called to be saints together with all those who in every place call upon the name of our Lord Jesus Christ" (1 Cor. 1:2). None of this is our own doing, because God called us to a holy calling "not because of our works but because of his own purpose and grace, which he gave us in Christ Jesus before the ages began" (2 Tim. 1:9). You probably made plans for today, contingent upon other people's plans (of course), but God's gracious purpose makes no accommodations. He made his plan to call you before the ages began.

God's mission has a single aim: to exalt Christ. In Ephesians, Paul is going to spell out what Christ's call, "Follow me," looks like for us. After he lays out foundational doctrine, Paul concludes in Ephesians 4:1–2, "I therefore, a prisoner for the Lord, urge you to walk in a manner worthy of the calling to which you have been called, with all humility and gentleness, with patience, bearing with one another in love."

Our hope is rock solid. It is not a human, fallible, "Oh, I just *hope* but am unable to bring it to pass. We shall see." This is no aimless, nebulous calling of "whatever floats your boat" uncertainty. We are not left with an ancient book of mere platitudes of ideals. No. We are following a person who yet lives, breathes, and acts. Peter says, "For to this you have been called, because Christ also suffered for you, leaving you an example, so that you might follow in his steps" (1 Pet. 2:21). The path we tread has been marked out for us by Jesus. God calls us to holiness, and we are driven along by a certain hope that will surely come to pass. When we understand God's call, we see our clear purpose, and we can more easily recognize and resist the world's pull toward functional aimlessness.

God's Glorious Inheritance

The second thing Paul wants us to know about God is that he has made us his glorious inheritance. This is a good word for us so that we don't live *functionally hopeless*.

Verse 18 says that God's inheritance is "in" the saints. Which saints? All the saints. Jews and Gentiles alike! No people group will be absent in heaven. God is the one who qualified us (all of us) "to share in the inheritance of the saints in light" (Col. 1:12). God has made us his inheritance, and we're (all!) looking forward "to an inheritance that is imperishable, undefiled, and unfading, kept in heaven" for us (1 Pet. 1:4). The suffering we endure in this present age (following Christ's steps) is evidence not that we have been abandoned or orphaned but that we are heirs of God and fellow heirs with Christ (Rom. 8:17). God is pleased to make us his own. Beloved, God is delighted to inherit his people.

When we can see with the eyes of our heart that God has made us his inheritance and there is a real, enduring, unfading, perfect inheritance being kept for us in heaven, we can more easily discern and resist the tug of the world toward functional hopelessness. All the body of Christ, that "great multitude that no one could number, from every nation, from all tribes and peoples and languages" (Rev. 7:9), will worship the Lamb and see his face (Rev. 22:3–4).

Immeasurably Great Power

The third thing Paul wants us to know about God is that he will wield his immeasurably great power on behalf of his children. Our hearts are strengthened when we see that we do not need to live as though we are *functionally helpless*. This particular prayer request is where Paul concentrates, for if God were powerless he could not make his call effectual or give us assurance that he will finally bring us home to our inheritance.

God's power is immeasurably great. Any religious person will agree with you on that statement. He makes volcanoes erupt, he directs dandelion seeds to their destination, and he is matchless in his might. But what makes our view of God's power distinctly Christian is that God has used his immeasurable power to do three cosmos-altering things: he raised Jesus from the dead; he seated Jesus at his right hand, putting all things under Jesus's feet; and he made Jesus head over all things for the church.

Death and evil are the two forces we have no power over. But Jesus, the God-man, has power over them. The man in heaven is in charge. This should blow our minds. The last Adam stands for us. Yes, we are alive in him. We have falling necks, as Nora Ephron said; we have no power over aneurysms; Alzheimer's happens; Angelina Jolie is trying to outrun her genetic propensity for cancer before it gets her; no man can tame his own tongue or thumbs; and what can we do in the face of such evil? We are impotent. But Christ is all-powerful. And he is for us.

As Jesus's crucified body lay entombed in the rock in the garden, God's immeasurably great power did not merely resuscitate him, like CPR or pushing a reset button. When God raised Jesus from the dead, he raised his body up immortal, a new creation, and glorified. Hebrews 2:5–9 tells us that when God exalted Jesus, he put everything in subjection to him, leaving nothing outside his control. (Though, at present, we do not yet see everything in subjection to him.)

When we see with the eyes of our heart that we are alive in Christ, we understand that God's immeasurably great power is toward us who believe. God in Christ conquered death and evil. When Jesus shared in our flesh and blood in his incarnation and then allowed himself to be killed, he destroyed the one who has the power of death (Satan). In doing so, he delivered all of us who through fear of death were subject to lifelong slavery (Heb. 2:14–15). This is very good news. Death and sin are the two powers over which mankind has no control. And now the man in heaven has control over both. Dominion over the works of God's hands has been retaken by the last Adam (Psalm 8). Take that, Satan. Of course God can deliver those who believe from death and evil!

With our eyes open to God's power toward us who believe, we can more easily discern the gravitational pull of the course of this world that speaks of our functional helplessness in the face of evil and our personal failure to be holy as God is holy.

So, What Are These "Powers"?

What are these "powers" that Ephesians speaks of? Perhaps you live in a sociocultural context where such powers are acknowledged and feared. Others of us live in a context where the existence of the powers is ignored, downplayed, demythologized, or explained as human entities. This letter, more than any other New Testament epistle, gives us the most information about how we are to consider these spiritual authorities. Rather than focusing on this subject in an isolated section in his letter, Paul includes references to the "powers" throughout Ephesians.

The powers are included in Paul's list of what is to be united in Christ according to God's plan—"things in heaven and things on earth" (Eph. 1:10). The risen Christ is exalted "far above all rule and authority and power and dominion, and above every name that is named, not only in this age but also in the one to come" (Eph. 1:21). While we were dead in our sin, we did not follow Christ, but we followed "the course of this world, following the prince of the power of the air, the spirit that is now at work in the sons of disobedience" (Eph. 2:2). The church is God's primary vehicle through which he confounds the powers as "through the church the manifold wisdom of God might now be made known to the rulers and authorities in the heavenly places" (Eph. 3:10). The Father is the source "from whom every family in heaven and on earth is named" (Eph. 3:15). As new creations in Christ, we are to specifically resist the temptation to sin in our anger "and give no opportunity to the devil" (Eph. 4:27). Our allegiance to Christ means that we, too, must resist his (and our) enemy as we "put on the whole armor of God, that [we] may be able to stand against the schemes of the devil" (Eph. 6:11). These efforts in our spiritual warfare are not against "flesh and blood, but against the rulers, against the authorities, against the cosmic powers over this present darkness, against the spiritual forces of evil in the heavenly places" (Eph. 6:12). Our faith in Jesus is our shield against the attacks of the enemy, which Paul describes as "flaming darts of the evil one" (Eph. 6:16). Paul's teaching and instruction concerning the unseen cosmic powers are throughout his letter, highlighting the fact that we live our lives on a cosmic stage.

A cohesive look at the powers as explained in Ephesians reveals that they occupy the heavenly realm, are subject to the Lord Jesus, influence "the course of this world" and unbelievers (including us when we were dead in our sin), and scheme against the sons and daughters of God. They are created by God and therefore not equal with God; they are dumbfounded by God's wisdom in what he is doing in his church, and we need protection from their influence.

In our present age of tumultuous wars, politics, persecution, pain, and uncertainty, it's hard to envision Christ's unmitigated rule over his enemies and these spiritual powers. How has God given Christ dominion and put all things under his feet (Ps. 8:6) as freedoms to practice our Christian faith are threatened even in Europe, Australia, and North America? How could his enemies be his footstool (Ps. 110:1) as bullets pierce through the bodies of his disciples in the Middle East, syncretism holds sway in South America, disciples have to hide in order to worship together in Asia, and churches burn in Africa?[3] "I think we're mostly 'not yet,' and I'm tired of hearing about the 'already,'" one weary soul confessed. Though Paul is focused on the "already" aspect here in this passage, we need not measure the influence one age has over another. Both are present concurrently, as the age to come has been inaugurated but not consummated. We live in the overlap of the ages—a time of tension and turmoil, the birth pangs of an old age that will give way to a glorious eternity.

Christ Fills His Church

Heavenly beings fly, stand, and fall down in worship in God's throne room. Jesus, the Son of Man, sits. According to his immeasurably great power, the Father put all things under the feet of Jesus and gave him as head over all things to the church, which is his body, the fullness of him who fills all in all (Eph. 1:22–23). This sounds like exceptionally superlative language from Paul, and it is. The parameters of "all" in these verses are namely that—*all*. Jesus cannot be described in terms that limit his sovereignty, authority, or fullness. Likewise, the church cannot be described in terms that limit her proximity to or affiliation with her head, Jesus. He is the head; she is his body. Christ fills his church.

A few paragraphs down in Ephesians 2, Paul hearkens back to the Old Testament to help us understand the significance of Christ filling his church. Before you look ahead at that passage, look at a couple hints of the revealed mystery from the Old Testament:

> When Yahweh's presence descended on the tabernacle among the Israelites in the wilderness: "Then the cloud covered the tent of meeting, and the glory of the LORD filled the tabernacle" (Ex. 40:34).

> When the Lord spoke with absolute certainty of his glory filling the earth: "But truly, as I live, and as all the earth shall be filled with the glory of the LORD" (Num. 14:21).

> When Solomon dedicated the newly constructed temple in Jerusalem: "As soon as Solomon finished his prayer, fire came down from heaven and consumed the burnt offering and the sacrifices, and the glory of the LORD filled the temple" (2 Chron. 7:1). "The priests could not stand to minister because of the cloud, for the glory of the LORD filled the house of the LORD" (1 Kings 8:11). And then Solomon wrote a song about longing for God's glory: "Blessed be his glorious name forever; may the whole earth be filled with his glory! Amen and Amen!" (Ps. 72:19).

When Habakkuk prophesied: "For the earth will be filled with the knowledge of the glory of the Lord as the waters cover the sea" (Hab. 2:14).

When Ezekiel was catapulted into an eschatological vision in which he saw the new-creation temple of God: "The Spirit lifted me up and brought me into the inner court; and behold, the glory of the Lord filled the temple" (Ezek. 43:5; cf. chaps. 40–48).

Adam and Eve dwelled in the glory of God's presence in the garden of Eden before they were exiled as part of their punishment for disobedience regarding the tree. Later in the Old Testament, God's presence primarily dwelled on earth in the tabernacle and the temple.

It would take the last Adam's obedience to his Father on another mount in another garden regarding another tree in order for man to enjoy the ongoing, glorious presence of God on earth. He is the Son who would say, "Not my will, but yours, be done" (Luke 22:42b). But still, we're not quite *there* yet. Read what Paul says in Ephesians 2:21–22, the passage I alluded to earlier:

. . . in whom the whole structure, being joined together, grows into a holy temple in the Lord. In him you also are being built together into a dwelling place for God by the Spirit.

The church is God's called people, and Jesus is not quite finished with us yet. This is a different kind of building campaign. Jesus himself is joining his called-out people together, growing us into a dwelling place. What is that dwelling place? We, the corporate people of God that transcend ethnicity and eras, are the dwelling place for God by the Spirit.[4] Jesus is the glory of God, and he fills his church through the gift of his Holy Spirit.

The presence of God is among us in the world through the presence of the church.

> After his resurrection and ascension, God's tabernacling presence descended in the form of the Spirit, so that those identified with Christ are included as part of the temple. The Father and Son, however, still reside in the heavenly temple and not on earth. Therefore, the temple's center of gravity during the church age is located in the heavenly realm but it has begun to invade the earthly through the Spirit in the church.[5]

No matter how comfortable we feel in our own skin, our own homes, and our own countries, we are not home. We are a pilgrim people even now. We are sojourners in the world (1 Pet. 2:11), expats until we reach the better country God is preparing for us (Heb. 11:16). The church does not yet enjoy the fullness of the triune God's presence. Our fulfilled enjoyment of God's fullness will occur when we finally "see his face" in the new heavens and the new earth, basking in his glorious presence. We haven't been home yet, but we're going there. When John was carried away in a vision, he saw the same new-creation temple that Ezekiel saw, which was "having the glory of God, its radiance like a most rare jewel, like a jasper, clear as crystal" (Rev. 21:11). The glory of God fills the city so profusely that "the city has no need of sun or moon to shine on it, for the glory of God gives it light, and its lamp is the Lamb" (Rev. 21:23).

Because God has (through Christ) given us his Spirit, we have every reason to believe that it will be granted to us to see the role of the church in this cosmic context. We have nothing to fear in this world, because our heavenly Bridegroom is ruling over all things for the sake of his bride, the church. Everything he does is for her, and so Paul wants us to know and appropriate "every spiritual blessing."

God's call on our lives is what gives us hope in the face of the everyday temptations to sin and despair of evil we see now. The glorious inheritance that God will give us causes us to set our faces like flint in the face of lesser pleasures. When we feel we have no strength in us at all to keep our hope or to desire God, we see that his immeasurably great power is what has kept us and will keep us until the end. This good news is spreading throughout the entire earth. The church is neither aimless and hopeless nor helpless. She must and will grow like a garden without borders to every corner of the earth. And then the fullness of the new creation will come. God has called us as his holy people, he has promised us a future, and the power of God will assuredly accomplish all his holy will. We "improvise" according to this reality.

Holy and blameless before him, here comes the bride of Christ! The gates of hell did not overcome her, and he kept her as his own until the very end, which is really, in the permanent light of the eternal city, a new beginning. To the praise of his glorious grace, "the upright shall behold his face" (Ps. 11:7). And we will dwell in the house of the Lord all the days of our life, gazing upon his beauty (Ps. 27:4).

The Spirit of God breathed out God's Word (2 Tim. 3:16), so it is fitting for us to breathe out the prayer he inspired Solomon to utter three thousand years ago:

> Blessed be his glorious name forever;
> > may the whole earth be filled with his glory!
> > > Amen and Amen! (Ps. 72:19)

Power toward Us

Paul prays that we would know Christ's exaltation over all things and his filling of all things. God raised Jesus from the dead and seated him at his right hand of power for an interminable length of time in a position that is far above all rule, authority, power, and dominion. Therefore, all rulers, authorities, powers, and dominions that are not in line with Christ's assertive reign are liable to dismantling, destruction, and everlasting conscious torment. That is what awaits all the evildoers who cling to their treasonous sin. Christ's filling all things corresponds to his authoritative will extending to every place, including hell. Every tear of those found faithful in Christ Jesus will be wiped away. And all who are found outside of Christ will justly endure his wrath.

The power and authority that are Christ's to punish his enemies are also his to make his enemies his friends. Even bloodthirsty predators who lie in wait for the blood of innocent people may yet repent of their sin and accept Jesus's offer of amnesty through his shed blood on the cross. Even those who are indifferent to Christ may yet be caught up in delight in his person and work. The gospel extends to more and more people every day, while Christ tarries and his judgment is still forthcoming.

God's power, which raised Jesus from the dead, enthroned him, and subjects all things to him, is what brings about and sustains the new-creation life. The heaving contractions of death pangs that would seek to destroy the eternal Son and usurp his power have been overturned by God's power. Instead, the grave bursts open in new life as the Son of Man rises from the dead and is exalted far above all things by the power of God. This is the same power of God that will assuredly raise all those united to Christ by faith (1 Cor. 6:14; 15:43; Phil. 3:21).

Christ's hands are steady and certain because he has been enthroned at God's right hand. His present enthronement in this place of utter power is evidence that he is able to accomplish what he is about right now as he is summing up all things in himself. Until the day comes (and only the Father knows when), we remain in the already–not yet time, precisely where the Father would have us in order that he might receive praise and his patience might effect opportunities for more of his lost children to repent and worship him. On this note, it is good to remember what "now" looks like: every imaginable rank or authority or title is underneath Christ in this age and the age to come, including death.

It also serves us to remember what "now" *could* look like: God powerfully raised Jesus from the dead, seated him at his right hand, and put all things under his feet. What would change about how we think about our potential to change if we knew "the immeasurable greatness of his power toward those who believe?" We live out of this reality. Let no believer in Jesus ever scoff, "Oh, her? She'll never change."

Being reminded of the greatness of God's power would have conjured up memories of recent events in the minds of the Ephesians. When the gospel spread through their city via the preaching of Paul, people repented en masse such that the economic scheme was significantly altered. People literally stopped buying idols and sacrifices to give to their city goddess, Diana. "Where your treasure is, there your heart will be also," Jesus said (Matt. 6:21). The Ephesians' pocketbooks were affected by their affection for Christ. They stopped keeping the idol economy afloat (Acts 19:23–27).

In a world that is hostile to the gospel, why would we want to preach a message that has no power unto salvation? But God has given us his gospel. According to the power of God in Christ, he has angled all the power in heaven and on earth to giving life to his children's dead souls and later resurrecting our earthly bodies into glorified ones. "All the manifold blessings, which rush like aggressively flowing rivers from the fountainhead of Christ, flow to the elect through the presence of the Spirit. God designed all this convergence. It was his plan by design."[6]

Change? Growth? Life? They are inevitable, friend. Oh, that we had eyes to see that we are alive in Christ! Don't take Paul's prayer for enlightened eyes with a grain of skeptical salt but with a mustard seed of faith.

Watch in the next chapter of Ephesians how Paul takes the truth of the exalted Christ in 1:20–23 and shows us something of what it means for us in 2:4–7. (And keep an eye out for later, in Ephesians 4:10, when Paul circles back to the theme of Christ's ascension and his filling of all things.) In the beginning, God created the heavens and the earth. Everything was *good*. But sin fractured the relationship the Creator had with his creation. Yet now the sincere petitions of Christians from every era are coming true in Christ as he is gathering up everything into submission to his will: "Our Father in heaven, hallowed be your name. Your kingdom come, your will be done, on earth as it is in heaven" (Matt. 6:9–10).

Let's look at the next chapter in Ephesians to see how Christ is doing God's will as he re-creates a new humanity in himself.

3

Zombies Raised to Life

God Resurrects a New Humanity

EPHESIANS 2:1-22

Over the course of human history many metaphors have been used to describe the Christian life. One such metaphor that has resounded through the centuries is walking. It is a common question to be asked among fellow brothers and sisters across the globe: "How is your walk with God?" Paul employs this walking metaphor as he paces back and forth between two kinds of people—those who are walking dead and those who are walking in new life. Once we were spiritual zombies (and walked accordingly), and now we are raised to life with Christ (and walk accordingly).

How Dead Were We?

Paul describes our spiritual zombie state in Ephesians 2:1–3:

> You were dead in the trespasses and sins in which you once walked, following the course of this world, following the prince of the power of the air, the spirit that is now at work in the sons of disobedience—among whom we all once lived in the passions of our flesh, carrying out the desires of the body and the mind, and were by nature children of wrath, like the rest of mankind.

We need to lose the mental image of our pre-Christian state as being a drowning person helplessly flailing about in the water, hoping upon hope that someone might throw us a life preserver. Outside of Christ we are, in fact, spiritual corpses rotting on the ocean floor among the silt and sludge. The mention of our deadness in transgressions *and* sins speaks to the comprehensive state of our lifeless soul. We are all (Jew and Gentile alike) spiritually dead outside of Christ, which is "the biblical diagnosis of fallen man in society everywhere."[1] Lest our fragile hearts sink within us, remember that Paul does not conjure up thoughts of our past in order to condemn us (as Satan does). Paul brings up the past so that we can see the matchless work of Christ in our lives.

Any whiff of death is meant to enliven our senses to God's great power in Christ to save us from all the things that enslaved us. Each of us, no matter how gilded or comfortable our cage seemed, was in compliant bondage to forces that were hell-bent on our destruction. Fallen men and women are rebels against the right and gracious authority of God, which means they have pledged allegiance to God's Enemy and follow his lead instead. And so it is with all who are yet outside of Christ. This is why we were the objects of God's just wrath (Eph. 2:3).

A threefold cord of destruction—the world, Satan, and our flesh—held us in bondage until we were rescued by Jesus.

Jesus gave himself for our sins to deliver us from the present evil age, according to the will of our God and Father (Gal. 1:4). What are this "present evil age" and the "course of this world"? The world is engulfed in a value system that corresponds to values that are not God's. The course of this world embodies every attitude, action, and affection that elicits the pleasure of God's Enemy. It's in the air. Do you hear God's name profaned on the street? Do you know any of God's image bearers who are being dehumanized? Do you know that the most helpless among us are being ravaged in the womb? Do you read in the news about the machines of injustice cranking out exploitation? Do you hear reports of wars waged according to ethnicity or gender? To follow the course of this world is to live in a purely material world; consume or be consumed is the enslaving law of worldly happiness.

The course of this world is pervasive, keeping the captives quiet with the morphine of temporary pleasure at the expense of their eternal souls. The course of this world is impersonal, not caring who is entrapped, but Satan, the god of this world, has personally blinded the minds of the unbelievers, to keep them from seeing the light of the gospel of the glory of Christ, who is the image of God (2 Cor. 4:4). While the course of this world is impersonal, God's enemy, Satan, is a personal being. His evil work is exclusively hell-bent on destroying what God has created, specifically and personally attacking men, women, children, and babies—God's image bearers. The third force over which fallen man has no control is the flesh. Paul isn't referring to our humanity—that which God created male and female and called "very good" (Gen. 1:31). The flesh is that sphere of our being that is inclined to sin, prone to wander, and wont to leave the God we love. Romans 8:8 says, "Those who are in the flesh cannot please God."

Who Will Rescue Us?

Until Jesus decisively frees us from following this present evil age, we are consumed in its centrifuge. Until Jesus effectively binds the strong man and his Spirit opens our eyes, we are blind to his satisfying glory. Until Jesus causes us to be born again and gives us his Spirit, we are in the flesh and not in the Spirit.

This is why we say that when the Holy Spirit conceived Jesus in Mary's womb it was an act of war. Jesus invaded this present evil age in which Satan steals, kills, and destroys, in order that we may have life and have it abundantly (John 10:10). Understanding the ministry of Christ on earth as one epic conflict really settles the dust on the old age. He came to the old age and comes into conflict with it because he aims to dismantle the powers and authorities and be exalted as head over all things. And this he has done. In his first coming, Jesus was tempted, rejected, tortured, and killed. The suffering servant conquered through his cross. And now, through his Spirit, he grows his body here on earth. The invasion of the new age (creation) into the old age continues as God's gospel of life is proclaimed through Christ's suffering church by the power of his Spirit in every corner of the earth.[2]

Paul writes, "You were dead" (Eph. 2:1). Being raised from death to life in Christ is so much more than mere behavior modification. Whereas before, we were dead *in* our sin, when we are co-crucified with Christ, we become dead *to* our sin. We are no longer bound to follow the course of this world, walking in our transgressions and sins. We are no longer oriented toward pleasing our flesh, dominating over other human beings, and offering our worship to vain things. The spell of darkness in this evil age has been broken through the body of Christ on the cross. The gates of heaven have been opened to us! And the path of life that is pleasing to the One who sits on the throne, a life marked by an inclination toward holiness, is now ours through Christ. By his Spirit, we can live out God's original design for us, blessing him and one another as we put to work all his creative power which works in us to imagine and develop new avenues by which we might glorify him. Salvation is so much more than mere "fire insurance" against hell. We are free to joyfully live out God's good design—free to walk in his ways.

And what about our rescue from the world, the Devil, and our flesh *today*? Careful students of Ephesians will notice the significance of the passages we've looked at so far in light of how Paul concludes the letter: with the need to wear our spiritual armor (6:10–20). "The overlap of the ages means that Christian existence is characterized by the warfare between them."[3] In Ephesians 1:20–22, we read an announcement about Christ's incontestable victory over his enemies. In Ephesians 2:5–6, we read about the insoluble connection between Christ and his people. Christ's authority over all things means that all whose allegiance lies with the rightful King have no need to fear. His power is for them in their everyday spiritual warfare as they stand firm against the gravitational pull of the course of this world, resist the Devil, and mortify the desires of their flesh.

But God

In Ephesians 2:4 we read what is perhaps one of the most cherished phrases in the Bible: "But God." It is the hinge of hope for desperately lost sinners like us. It is the climax of every gospel presentation. It leaves behind it a swelling wake of grace that will continue to ripple into eternity.

> But God, being rich in mercy, because of the great love with which he loved us.

The world with all its birth pangs of tribulation will continue until the appointed time on the course that has been predetermined by its Creator, who is the holy judge of all the earth. But to all those on whom God sets his great love—those people will escape the wrath of God because of the rich mercy of God. Those two small words in the English language, "But God," are pregnant with eternal significance and hope. One can almost feel the upheaval of relief as hope bursts forth out of Ephesians 2:4. The idea held forth in that verse holds your gaze as a glimpse of the real joy to which all other joys are but a distant echo, as J. R. R. Tolkien put it.

So we behold the glory of God in his rich mercy and his great love, but to what end? Why? We hang onto the "But God" of the gospel by faith through grace, because in that gospel we trace the echo back to the source of all things. We find Joy himself. And O, what kindness we have been shown by God in Christ Jesus! For *we were not even looking for him* when he found us. Our deadness is interrupted by rich mercy, and we are raised to life in the throes of un-looked-for upheavals of joy. This kind of tasting and seeing of God's goodness tells us that there is more to life than what we can taste and see. Then we become hungry for more and more of it. And our eyes will not stop searching the horizon of eternity, hoping to catch a glimpse of the Beloved who promised that he would return for his bride.

In the meantime, until his longed-for appearing, we wait. And in our waiting we *live. We live!* First, we are granted the mercy of living outside the garden of Eden even though we had been dead in our sin. Second, God's grace sees to it that those who are "in Christ" are made alive together with Christ (v. 5). The soul is raised to life; we are raised up with Christ and seated with him in the heavenly places in Christ Jesus (v. 6).

Seated with Christ in the Morning Commute

Ephesians sheds light on a biblical understanding of the hip phrase "authentic Christian life." When you are living an "authentic" Christian life, it doesn't make sense to live as though you belong to the world. You should live in a manner worthy of the calling to which you have been called. It is neither fitting nor appropriate to go your way as an orphan in the world if God has adopted you. Living like a spiritual zombie is an expression of the irrationality of our sin nature and is symptomatic of our profuse confusion. We must unlearn the ways of the world and "learn Christ" (Eph. 4:20). Our obedience to God is not the kindling for the fire of our salvation but the heat emanating from the fire that God started and fuels. Authenticity, for the Christian, is a heart posture of humility toward God and others. We have been raised up with Christ.

I hope that I will never forget when the reality of verse 6 began to dawn on me. The traffic was particularly awful on my way to pick up my daughter from school. Congestion was so bad that I picked up my phone to dial a friend of mine, a teacher at the school, to ask her to go get my daughter when the bell rang so she wouldn't be sent to the principal's office to wait for her late mom. It was about forty degrees Celsius (that is, about well over one hundred degrees Fahrenheit), the little children in the car were anxious to be done waiting in traffic, and I was daydreaming about owning a helicopter. On the car's CD player,

I had been listening to the Ephesians 1 track on repeat (which is a very handy way to commit Scripture to memory). Verse 6 cut through the fog in my brain, and I heard loud and clear what God's Word said about me: "You have been raised up with Christ and seated with him in the heavenly places." I realized that as tangible as that gridlock was and as loud as the honking cars were, there is simultaneous reality that trumps all the transient, temporal things of this earth. I might have been stuck in traffic in that moment, experiencing all the frustration and angst that accompanies that sort of situation. But there was no way that this circumstance could touch the reality of my being in Christ, raised up and seated with him in heaven. There I was, sitting in my Kia Carnival minivan, which might have been true for about sixty minutes. But being in Christ is where I am currently and where I will be sixty billion years from now.

What is most astonishing about Ephesians 2:6 is not merely that this is where God has placed us in Christ, but also *why*. Why does God do this? He does this because of his rich mercy and great love, yes. But, specifically, he does this "so that in the coming ages he might show the immeasurable riches of his grace in kindness toward us in Christ Jesus" (v. 7). All our striving in the sins in which we once walked, all the chains with which we had been shackled by this world, all the fleshly passions that held us captive, all the holy wrath that we justly deserved—all of this is exchanged for a show unlike any show we have ever enjoyed before. The transaction is all wrought of grace. In the place of the eternal death we deserved, we get to enjoy the immeasurable riches of God's grace throughout the coming ages. God's riches and kindness in Christ are immeasurable because Christ himself is immeasurable. We'll certainly need the entirety of eternity to experience all his grace, because his grace toward us is boundless. If you've ever wondered why heaven lasts for eternity, that's why.

What does Christ's ascension mean for us while we're waiting and hoping for heaven? Whereas Adam's sin had closed off our access to fellowship with God, Jesus has made a way physically through his own body. Through Christ our representative head, we possess all of his blessings in the heavenly places.

In our waiting, we live out of this reality. We *walk* out of this reality of being in Christ now and forever. The grace that saves us is the gift of God ("not a result of works, so that no one may boast," v. 9). Boasting is completely out of place in the new humanity in Christ, except, of course, boasting in the cross. Our adoption into God's forever family is not owing to anything we have done but owing to our Father setting his love on us. Boasting in ourselves is replaced by glorying in Jesus and what he has done. Since our salvation is a gift, we do not hold it over others' heads, as though the gift were a testament to our righteousness.

Them Dry Bones Gonna Walk Around

The Lord showed Ezekiel a vision explaining why he was going to regenerate his covenant people and how he was going to do it. So he took him to a place that was brimming with death: a valley grave filled with very dry bones. These were the bones of God's covenant people. Led around and among a valley filled with dry bones, Ezekiel was asked this question: "Son of man, can these bones live?" He answered well: "O Lord GOD, you know" (Ezek. 37:3). Then God commanded, "Prophesy over these bones, and say to them, 'O dry bones, hear the word of the LORD'" (v. 4). Ezekiel prophesied as he was commanded; the word of the Lord went forth; and bones rattled together, followed by ligaments, fat, flesh, and skin. But these people were zombies without lights in their eyes. There was no breath in them.

God commanded Ezekiel again: "Prophesy to the breath; prophesy, son of man, and say to the breath, Thus says the Lord GOD: Come from the four winds, O breath, and breathe on these slain, that they may live" (Ezek. 37:9). So he did, and when breath entered their bodies, the exceedingly great army came alive and they all stood on their feet. God explained that he was going to open the graves of his people and raise them up: "And I will put my Spirit within you, and you shall live, and I will place you in your own land. Then you shall know that I am the LORD; I have spoken, and I will do it, declares the LORD" (v. 14).

And now this new-creation reality of regeneration is for the believing Gentiles as well as the believing Jews. The Ephesians "were dead in the trespasses and sins" (Eph. 2:1; cf. 1:5). But God "made us alive together with Christ" (v. 5). The "us" Paul is referring to includes both Jews and Gentiles. God made us alive together, raising us up with Christ (v. 6). Even now, as the gospel spreads through every ethnic barrier that was torn down in Christ, you can hear the bones rattling. Jesus breathes his Spirit into our lifeless souls, and we are raised up. God said that he would place his covenant people in their own land so that we would know that he is the Lord (Ezek. 37:14). So he has seated us with Christ in the heavenly places so that in the coming ages he might show us the immeasurable riches of his grace in kindness toward us in Christ Jesus (Eph. 2:6–7).

Those dry bones, that exceedingly great army, are God's workmanship (i.e., God's new creation). We are the body of Christ, that body whose food is the word of the Lord, who are held together by the joints and sinews that God has provided. Our dry bones are enlivened by the very breath of God's Spirit— his new creation created for good works—that we should walk around in them (Eph. 2:10).[4]

A New Cadence

By grace through faith we are saved, and by grace through faith we walk in the good works God has prepared for us. The dark ways we followed and the death in which we lived are exchanged with this: walking in light and good works that point to the fact that we are living out of the reality of being saved by grace through faith.

Whereas we once walked in sin (Eph. 2:2), we now walk in the good works God has prepared for us (v. 10). The calling and ministry of the gospel are ours for the walking in. This isn't a new calling or ministry for God's people. When the Lord gave his perfect law to Israel, Moses spoke to the people and summarized what that law would mean: "And now, Israel, what does the LORD your God require of you, but to fear the LORD your God, to walk in all his ways, to love him, to serve the LORD your God with all your heart and with all your soul" (Deut. 10:12). Many faithful (and many forgetful) generations later, King Solomon built a glorious temple, and the glory of the Lord filled that place, and he prayed and dedicated the temple saying,

> O LORD, God of Israel, there is no God like you, in heaven above or on earth beneath, keeping covenant and showing steadfast love to your servants who walk before you with all their heart. (1 Kings 8:23)

There is no God like the God of Israel! But who can stand before the Holy One? Malachi asks,

But who can endure the day of his coming, and who can stand when he appears? For he is like a refiner's fire and like fullers' soap. (Mal. 3:2)

Jesus Christ is the answer to Malachi's question, as he is the one through whom we can stand in the presence of God's consuming fire. "He chose us in [Christ] before the foundation of the world, that we should be holy and blameless before him" (Eph. 1:4). Jude's benediction rings with the eternal gladness that is ours through Jesus Christ:

Now to him who is able to keep you from stumbling and to present you blameless before the presence of his glory with great joy, to the only God, our Savior, *through Jesus Christ our Lord*, be glory, majesty, dominion, and authority, before all time and now and forever. Amen. (Jude 24–25)

Through the gospel, hearts of flesh replace hearts of stone as ancient prophecies come true. When God calls together his people, he says he "will give them one heart, and a new spirit I will put within them. I will remove the heart of stone from their flesh and give them a heart of flesh, that they may walk in my statutes and keep my rules and obey them. And they shall be my people, and I will be their God" (Ezek. 11:19–20). How is it that former "children of wrath" could walk in a manner pleasing to the Lord? "He has told you, O man, what is good; and what does the LORD require of you but to do justice, and to love kindness, and to walk humbly with your God?" (Micah 6:8). What the Lord requires of us, to humbly walk in his way, he supplies.

Remembering our resurrected status in Christ is both the foundation and the assurance our fragile hearts need when we feel we are powerless to please the Lord in our obedience to him. Here in Ephesians 2:10 we see that God has planned that we would do precisely that—faithfully walk in the good works he has prepared for us.[5] As his plan assuredly will come to pass, we find fresh motivation to walk in a manner worthy of the gospel we have believed.

Understanding Paul's meaning in chapter 2 is utterly critical for how we understand the rest of his letter. Here are a few examples. Because of the nature of the gospel and the character of our God, it only makes sense, then, that Paul urges us to walk in a manner worthy of our calling (Eph. 4:1). Our walking has a new cadence; we don't march to the beat of our own drum anymore. Our former way of life was marked by futility in thinking (Eph. 4:17). But we've been given the mind of Christ! So we use it. We use the mind of Christ to think of ways we can imitate God, as his beloved children (Eph. 5:1). Like Father, like sons and daughters. Our elder Brother made a way for us to be adopted into God's family when he "gave himself up for us" on the cross. So we walk in love, in the way of our Savior, which is a fragrant offering and sacrifice to God (Eph. 5:2). Whereas we once fumbled about in darkness because we were darkness, we now walk as children of light because we are light in the Lord (Eph. 5:8).

Of course, it follows that we would be wise to "look carefully" after the way that we walk, living out the implications of what it means to be a new humanity in Christ (Eph. 5:15). Ephesians spells out what our unity in Christ means, which is far more than the anemic version of unity that is defined by agreeability. The body of Christ is a reality that is stronger, farther reaching, and more shocking than mere agreeability.

One New Man without Walls

When we say that "we have unity in Christ," we mean that we as Christ's people *are* united in Christ. Jesus has created "one new man," shared his inheritance with this new humanity, and works to build us together into a dwelling place for God by the Spirit (Eph. 2:11–22). The presence of the church—the people of God gathered together—is evidence of Christ's victory over the cosmic powers. As God chose to dwell in the Most Holy Place in the tabernacle and the temple, he chooses now to dwell in and among his people gathered. The people are the temple.

It makes sense that we as the new humanity would reflect his glory, purity, humility, kindness, grace, and love. God has made his dwelling among us, and his Spirit lives in us, and we live out this reality in the way we walk. Paul argues this when he quotes from Leviticus 26:12:

> What agreement has the temple of God with idols? For we are the temple of the living God; as God said, "I will make my dwelling among them and walk among them, and I will be their God, and they shall be my people." (2 Cor. 6:16)

In Ephesians 2:17 Paul quotes an ancient prophecy: "Peace, peace, to the far and to the near . . . and I will heal him" (Isa. 57:19). The reconciliation of Jews and Gentiles is in view here.[6] Not even walls can stop Jesus from building his church, those who are chosen in him from eternity past. The dividing wall of the barrier that Jesus broke down is the part of the law that divided the Jews from the Gentiles. With the symbols, ceremonies, and customs of national Israel's laws abolished, the believing Jews and believing Gentiles could both become "true Israelites" without needing to adopt signs such as circumcision or food laws. The one thing that distinguishes true people of God is Jesus Christ. In the place of that broken-down wall, Jesus himself is placed as the cornerstone (Eph. 2:20). He is creating in himself a new humanity, joining together Jew and Gentile,

Eritrean and Papuan, Emirati and Italian. The whole lot of us, in all our varied colors, sizes, and accents, are growing into a holy temple in the Lord (Eph. 2:21).

But how does a temple *grow*? It grows like a garden, one that feeds on a very specific food and is pruned in a very specific way:

> The church as a temple fulfills God's intention for the expanding Garden-temple seen in Genesis 1:28 (in the context of Gen. 2–3). . . . This Garden temple will grow by means of the word of God in a context of suffering. This temple must expand in this way and fill the earth through believers as Christ's witnesses to the ends of the earth (Acts 1:8).[7]

We see here that no dividing wall or obstacle—not even persecution—can contain the church as she spreads to cover the whole earth.

The Gospel Changes Everything

God is so pleased with what his Son has done and the effects of his Son's work in and through us. Jesus, who became the incarnate God in the flesh, "tabernacled" among us. He is *yet* God in the flesh and will forever remain embodied in our flesh. Through faith in Jesus the people of God are gathered together into the "body of Christ," which is the temple of the Holy Spirit (1 Cor. 3:16–17; Eph. 2:19–22). Through the indwelling Holy Spirit, Jesus dwells in us and among us so that he can claim, "Behold, I am with you always, to the end of the age" (Matt. 28:20). Christ is the ultimate Adam, the "household manager," who is uniting all things in himself (Eph. 1:10) as he infallibly puts the cosmos back together (e.g., tearing down the dividing wall between Jew and Gentile, among other home-reno tasks.)

The Bible points us to look forward to the end of the age when there will be a garden city not made with human hands, and in that place the throne of God and of the Lamb will be in it, and his servants will worship him (Rev. 22:1–5). We will see God's face because he will dwell among us forever and ever. We go from hiding in the garden for the shame of having sinned against the Lord, to walking humbly with the Lord. The single most mind-blowing, life-altering reality of being in Christ is that we no longer need to hide ourselves from the presence of the Lord God; in Christ we may walk with God in perfect fellowship now, and ultimately forever in the garden city that is to come (Gen. 3:8).

We need to hear this truth as individuals who are individually accountable to our Creator, and we need to hear it as a plural "we." The kind of walking that befits the calling we, the church, have been given is for our freedom. God has marked us for holiness. I love how Mark Dever ties all of these ideas together:

> Satan wants us to think of holiness as bondage, when it's really freedom. Your church and mine, by reflecting God's character, become lights that shine in a very dark world. One holy person can draw people's attention. But a holy community creates a picture of humanity that people have only dreamed of.[8]

Do these ideas sound like a dream you once had, which now seems distant, evaporating like mist in the heat of the world's pressures and anxieties? Let your heart be thrilled, then, to hear God's pleasure in what his Son has done:

> I heard a loud voice from the throne saying, "Behold, the dwelling place of God is with man. He will dwell with them,

and they will be his people, and God himself will be with them as their God." (Rev. 21:3)

Right and good responses to this truth are to tremble with the fear of God, wonder as you peer into God's Word, dance and shout aloud for joy, be dumbstruck into silence, and weep at the mercy that has found you. What kind of God would do this—adopt children of wrath into his own family through the sacrifice of his one and only Son?

Do you believe that God has done this? Does God's loud voice of joyful exultation in his Son ring loud and clear when the voices of the world assault you with lies? Have you been given a heart of flesh that beats strong to the truth of God's joy in being your God? What characterizes the way you walk? Christian, do you realize that God's Spirit tabernacles in you and that you are joined together with all God's people everywhere so that you might be priests who dwell in God's presence? Does your priestly status before the Lord of the earth inform the way you feel, think, do, speak, and write? Do we grieve the reality of the sin that yet entangles us and enslaves those around us? Do we long to see "the kingdom of the world . . . become the kingdom of our Lord and of his Christ" (Rev. 11:15)?

May God give us eyes to see and ears to hear and everything we need to walk in his way.

4

Mystery Revealed

We Are Members of the Same Body

EPHESIANS 3:1-21

Faster and faster, the world seems to be spinning out of control. Talk of culture wars and rumors of nuclear wars are in the air. With the help of the digital revolution, it seems that the world's stage is set for a mere second before history is forgotten. In the middle of it all, questions of the church's relevance fly at us from the West and the East. The West says our archaic dogma is the mark of the bigot. The East is preoccupied with internal apocalyptic threats. Inside evangelicalism there are some who cry out, "Abandon ship!" Others plead, "Save our ship!" And others argue, "Is a ship the best metaphor? Because I prefer *hospital*. And definitely not *library*. I mean, really. We need to nail down our favorite nickname and make sure the rest of Christendom gets the memo."

Collin Hansen writes in his provocative book *Blind Spots: Becoming a Courageous, Compassionate, and Commissioned Church*, "Jesus wants to illumine our blind spots so we can see our differences as opportunities."[1] This shouldn't sound unsettling to us, but it does. Our differences are just as much a manifestation of God's wisdom as is our unity. In this chapter we'll see how the church is both the light of the world (Matt. 5:14) and of the cosmos (Eph. 3:10). The stage is set—the grand theater spotlight is focused on the church. I wonder if any of us will be surprised to see who is being harassed by the brilliance of the church's little light—and who is irresistibly drawn toward the warmth.

Mystery Theater: The Spectacle of the Church

Ephesians 3 answers those questions of relevance by throwing back the curtains on a mystery. In eternity past, the mind of the triune God conceived of the script for a grand megadrama. This script is revealed in Scripture and specifically in Ephesians 3:9–10. He created the universe to be the cosmic stage for the glory of his Son, and he predestined the church as the leading lady. In this drama, the mystery of the church is like one big aha moment, and it reveals God's wisdom to those who inhabit the spiritual realm. You could say that the church is God's cosmic *booyah*.

From the various stipulations of the covenants, sacrifices, feasts, and temple worship, to the priests, judges, kings, and prophets—these "copies" give way to the "true things" (Heb. 9:23–24) and shine one collective spotlight on the eternal Son. God realized his eternal purpose in Christ Jesus—in his incarnation, sinless life, sacrificial death, triumphant resurrection, and ascension back into heaven, the gift of his Spirit, and his continued work on earth through his body, which includes believing Jews *and* Gentiles (Eph. 3:6). Stott explains, "The Christian mysteries are truths which, although beyond human discovery, have been revealed by God and so now belong openly to the whole church. More simply, *mysterion* is a truth hitherto hidden from human knowledge but now disclosed by the revelation of God."[2]

When God turned on the technicolor through Paul's preaching to the Gentiles, it was kinda crazy, to say the least. Followers of Yahweh have always been enjoined to make his name known in all the earth, from the first man and woman until now. Glimpses into the mystery of the church can be spotted all over the Old Testament, leading up to the big reveal.[3] One of the first glimpses we see is when God called a moon-worshiping pagan named Abram and his barren wife, Sarai, and made his covenant with them:

> Go from your country and your kindred and your father's house to the land that I will show you. And I will make of you a great nation, and I will bless you and make your name great, so that you will be a blessing. I will bless those who bless you, and him who dishonors you I will curse, and in you all the families of the earth shall be blessed. (Gen. 12:1–3)

Jesus left heaven and his Father's house to the land he created. God is making of him a great nation of men and women from every tribe. The Father blessed him and has given him the name above every name. In Christ we are blessed, and those who deny him are cursed. Indeed, all the families of the earth are blessed through faith in Jesus.

Every Jew knew about the "latter days" spoken of in Isaiah 2:2–4 in which "all the nations" and "many peoples" would worship the God of Jacob at his holy mountain in his holy city. They knew that God would rule the nations as they "beat their swords into plowshares, and their spears into pruning hooks." But the gospel announcement to the Gentiles through Paul—that Jews and Gentiles were united into one nation in Christ—was radical. Gentiles as coheirs? As part of God's con-corporate people? As co-sharers in his promises? This was Paul's message (see also Acts 21:17–26; 22:21; Col. 4:3).[4] Believing Jews and Gentiles worship the God of Jacob in the Spirit, wherever they live, having come to Christ crucified on a mount outside the city. Followers of Christ from every tribe now lay down their weaponry of skepticism, superiority, and hate toward one another. Instead, they use the gifts of the Spirit to build up one another in love, even as God is building them into his dwelling place. Heirs, members, sharers—all are in one body of Christ for all.

Jesus Turns Us into His Father's Big, Big House

When Jesus came upon the temple and saw that the outer court was filled with money-changers, pigeon hawkers, goat sellers, and all manner of merchants who used the temple worship for financial gain, he kicked them all out. Frustrated and upset for having their way of life interrupted, the people basically said to Jesus, "Who do you think you are?" (i.e., "What sign do you show us for doing these things?," John 2:18). Jesus answered famously, "Destroy this temple, and in three days I will raise it up" (John 2:19). We know that he was referring to his own body, because he was raised from the dead after three days. But how often do we remember that Christ's resurrection was the foundation for our corporate body, the church? Recall Ephesians 2:6, how God "raised us up with him and seated us with him in the heavenly places in Christ Jesus."

And look again at Ephesians 2:19–22, the passage G. K. Beale calls "one of the most explicit descriptions of the church as the temple in all of the New Testament":[5]

> So then you are no longer stranger and aliens, but you are fellow citizens with the saints and members of the household of God, built on the foundation of the apostles and prophets, Christ Jesus himself being the cornerstone, in whom the whole structure, being joined together, grows into a holy temple in the Lord. In him you also are being built together into a dwelling place for God by the Spirit.

This peculiar image of a growing building is the cosmic reality of the church. The metaphors mix together to show us the manifold wisdom of God. Jesus, the cornerstone who was raised, is building his church out of people from every tribe and nation and has made us a kingdom and priests unto his Father (Matt. 16:18; Rev. 5:9–10). We, the church, have become the reality to which the shadows in the Old Testament pointed.

No wonder Jesus was so angry when he saw how commercialism, materialism, and greed had seeped into the outer court of the Jerusalem temple. The outer court was specially designated as "a house of prayer for all peoples," like he said (Isa. 56:3–8). And the priestly Jews were to use that area of the temple to invite and welcome the Gentiles into the grace of God. This was in keeping with God's mission-loving heart:

> "And the foreigners who join themselves to the LORD,
>   to minister to him, to love the name of the LORD,
>   and to be his servants,
> everyone who keeps the Sabbath and does not profane it,
>   and holds fast my covenant—
> these I will bring to my holy mountain,

and make them joyful in my house of prayer;
their burnt offerings and their sacrifices
    will be accepted on my altar;
for my house shall be called a house of prayer
    for all peoples."
The Lord GOD,
    who gathers the outcasts of Israel, declares,
"I will gather yet others to him
    besides those already gathered." (Isa. 56:6–8)

The inclusion of believing Gentiles into the people of God was not unprecedented. Jesus's serious response to those who would hinder such people from sincere faith and inclusion in the temple worship gives us reason for pause. Since the mystery of Christ, "which was not made known to the sons of men in other generations as it has now been revealed to his holy apostles and prophets by the Spirit" (Eph. 3:5), is now made clear to us, how can we in good conscience ignore two billion unreached people? How can we in good conscience scoff at the members of the church that meets on the other side of the tracks? How can we in good conscience prefer ourselves and our comfort zones when God gives us opportunities to suffer for his sake and "present our bodies as living sacrifices" (Rom. 12:1) in the "outer court" of this world for the sake of those who are not yet gathered? How can we in good conscience neglect our priestly duty of praying that all the nations might come in so that the Lamb would receive the reward of his suffering?

God is bringing about the fulfillment of the Isaiah 56:3–8 prophecy as believing Jews and believing Gentiles alike come to Christ. We—Kazakhs, Kurds, Chechen, Chero, Chadic, Caucasian, and Jews—come to the city of the living God together. We journey together toward the heavenly Jerusalem and to innumerable angels in festal gathering, and we answer the "roll call" at the assembly of the firstborn who are enrolled in heaven. Together we come to Jesus, who mediates for us this new covenant through his blood (Heb. 12:22–24). Christians are not a geographically oriented people who are required to pilgrimage to a holy place on this earth, for God has given us his Spirit to dwell in our hearts. We sojourn throughout the earth, following the Spirit's leading as he searches out the sheep who are not yet in the fold. Jesus said, "I have other sheep that are not of this fold. I must bring them also, and they will listen to my voice. So there will be one flock, one shepherd" (John 10:16). The calling of Jesus is by his Word, and we bring his Word to every sheep no matter if that sheep looks or sounds different from us and eats or smells differently than we do. Our good conscience glows with satisfying joy at this calling. The Spirit will lead us to consciously revel in this joy.

We welcome everybody, just as we have been welcomed in Christ. And when others accept Christ's welcome by faith through grace into this new covenant, he turns them into fellow welcomers, just like us. The guest now hosts, inviting others to trust Christ the living stone (1 Pet. 2:4). The scattered stones now join together with one another, being built up as a spiritual house (1 Pet. 2:5a). The people who needed atonement now offer spiritual sacrifices acceptable to God through Christ Jesus (1 Pet. 2:5b). Those who gloried in their ethnicity now glory in Christ's blood alone. Those who boasted in their pedigree now humble themselves, having been made a royal priesthood. Those who walked in darkness now shine light into the darkness. The witnessed-to now witness, speaking of the riches of Christ. "The mark of the true church is always to be outward-looking and expanding God's presence and not obsessively introspective."[6]

Isaiah prophesied that a time was coming "to gather all nations and tongues. And they shall come and shall see my glory. . . . And some of them also I will take for priests and for Levites" (Isa. 66:18, 21). God is doing this among us even now:

> But you are a chosen race, a royal priesthood, a holy nation, a people for his own possession, that you may proclaim the excellencies of him who called you out of darkness into his marvelous light. (1 Pet. 2:9)

The mystery hidden for ages has now been revealed: God has chosen men and women from all nations to be indwelt by his Spirit and joined together to his Son. Since the angels who see the face of God continually have their curiosity piqued by the existence of his multiethnic church (1 Pet. 1:12), and the evil powers are confounded by the bride (Eph. 3:10), we would do well to quiet our own hearts in wonder. The mission of God is to bring about the filling of all things in his Son through the witness of this multicolored church. May his Spirit align our hearts with his.

Your New Heartbeat

If racism isn't a touchy subject in your circle of friends or in your church, or if protests against racial injustice seem as though they're half a world away from your everyday life, take a glance at the comment threads in the online local newspaper. For some reason the vitriol and venom tend to collect like cesspools at the bottom of the page, especially under articles about ethnicity-driven violence. Some of us may not need to skim the comment threads but can just listen for our neighbors' unfiltered comments.

One morning after one of our church potlucks I sat in my neighbor's living room. She confessed to me that all night long she had had her face pressed up against her window, staring into our courtyard. "All night I saw the Africans, the Asians, the Westerners—everyone. They were bringing food and eating together. Why would you want to do that?"

I saw the open door for the gospel, and I walked through it explaining that Jesus broke down the dividing wall of hostility among us and made us into one people.

She sneered. "There are men and women in my religion all over the world. But they are not my brother or my sister. I would never eat with . . ." And she proceeded to name the people groups she despised. All of us—from those who are openly racist to those who are subtly ethnocentric—need to have new hearts in order to love this design that was dreamed up by God in eternity past.

Let your heart beat with a new heart; that's how our heart will be aligned with God's heart. God's Word tells us that the human heart is deceitful above all things and desperately sick (Jer. 17:9; also see our discussion on Eph. 2:1–9). It is a liar and not to be trusted. That's why you need a new heart—one God provides through his new creation in you at the moment of your conversion. God replaces our heart of stone that is prone to wander—that conglomerate of lies more alluring than "guilt-free" dessert and more asinine than clickbait headlines—and replaces it with a heart of flesh that is prone to love him. And he gives us his Spirit to live in us, a truth Paul introduced us to in Ephesians 1:14.

The gift of the Spirit is no mere I.O.U. from God to cash in on later. No, he is the reality of the new-creation life that we are already beginning to taste. Does your soul pant for God as a deer pants for water (Ps. 42:1)? Do you long for the pure spiritual milk of God's Word like a newborn longs for its mother's milk (1 Pet. 2:2)? Do you groan inwardly, longing to be clothed in your eternal body (Rom. 8:23; 2 Cor. 5:2, 4)? Does your heart tremble and beat faster when you wonder what it will be like to toss aside your dim mirror and see him face-to-face, knowing fully (1 Cor. 13:12)? That rumbling, aching hunger you sense for the new creation is but the beginning. It is the Spirit, waking up your spiritual taste buds to taste and see that Jesus is good. The Spirit has been given to you fully—God has not given him to you only in part. And when your earthly tent is raised incorruptible in the resurrection, you will freely enjoy the glory of God without the hindrance of remaining sin.

All our soul panting, spiritual-milk craving, inner groaning, and heart thrills are informed and enhanced by God's Word. Even today, will you, by faith, follow the Spirit's prompting to feed on God's Word as Jesus did, to let him make your soul's mouth water at the banquet that is unlike anything you've ever seen? "I will feast the soul of the priests with abundance, and my people shall be satisfied with my goodness, declares the LORD" (Jer. 31:14). That chapter in Jeremiah leads up to the glorious new-covenant declaration that Yahweh thunders forth with an astonishing resonance of hope for a sinful people:

> For this is the covenant that I will make with the house of Israel after those days, declares the LORD: I will put my law within them, and I will write it on their hearts. And I will be their God, and they shall be my people. (Jer. 31:33)

Through the prophet Ezekiel, God tells us exactly how he is going to do that:

> I will give you a new heart, and a new spirit I will put within you. And I will remove the heart of stone from your flesh and give you a heart of flesh. (Ezek. 36:26)

The first way we honor God in having a heart like his is to be born again. As moral and kind as many nonbelievers are, they do not have the new heart and the new spirit that they need in order to have a heart like his. This new heart and the indwelling Holy Spirit are gifts we do not deserve. If you are in Christ, just pause. Now be conscious of your eyes blinking. Most of us—corrective lenses or not—usually just look around at things because it's just what we do. Well, God in his grace has opened the eyes of our heart to see wonderful things in his law. Now that's just what we new creations in Christ do. God turned spiritual zombies into tasters and seers of the riches of Christ—to the praise of his glorious grace.

Searching Out the Unsearchable Riches of Christ

Included in the "riches of Christ" is every spiritual blessing we read about in Ephesians 1 and 2. And they are literally unsearchable! That word *unsearchable* means "not to be tracked out." We have no alternative but to be dumbfounded that God would elect guilty sinners such as us to be the recipients of Christ's riches. God is the one "who does great things and unsearchable, marvelous things without number" (Job 5:9).

> Oh, the depth of the riches and wisdom and knowledge of God! How unsearchable are his judgments and how inscrutable his ways! (Rom. 11:33)

Because we are finite creatures and will always be finite creatures, we are not able to comprehend God's inscrutable ways. Even if you dove deep into your Scripture-grounded, Spirit-empowered imagination and tried to bring up the biggest, most glorious picture of the riches of Christ, you wouldn't have even scratched the surface. We cannot track out every implication of

God's electing love toward us, but this does not hinder our joy. Not in the least! John Stott said that "what is certain about the wealth Christ has and gives is that we shall never come to an end of it."[7]

Just one of the implications of Christ's riches is that he has made it so that we will never be separated from his love. Even when Paul spells out this aspect of Christ's unsearchable riches, he has to use a blanket statement at the beginning and the end— "in all these things" and "nor anything else in all creation."

> No, in all these things we are more than conquerors through him who loved us. For I am sure that neither death nor life, nor angels nor rulers, nor things present nor things to come, nor powers, nor height nor depth, nor anything else in all creation, will be able to separate us from the love of God in Christ Jesus our Lord. (Rom. 8:37–39)

Indeed, "the steadfast love of the LORD never ceases; his mercies never come to an end; they are new every morning; great is your faithfulness" (Lam. 3:22–23). We have cause for increasing joy in Christ as we revel in his mercy, and we smile because we know it is always morning somewhere.

Every other love we experience in this life just falls so short. Sometimes my iced coffee goes lukewarm. Sometimes my darling children annoy me. Sometimes my friends don't respond to my needs the way I thought they would. Sometimes my husband thinks of himself before he thinks of me. While I remain in this body that is beset with sin, I'm tempted to live as though the world revolves around me, and I am regularly disappointed. But when this perishable body is raised imperishable (1 Cor. 15:42), I will be free from sin, and I will see finally and forever how the cosmos is centered on Christ. And no one will be able to dampen my joy ever again. It's a good thing that eternity will last forever, because it will take us that long to experience all the dimensions of Christ's love for us.

There are no hoarders in the kingdom. When we understand this truth—that we have been richly blessed in Christ—we realize that this truth is for sharing. Jesus, our Good Shepherd, never leaves us wanting (Ps. 23:1). He leads us to green pastures that we could never (and would never) dwell in on our own. Christians love to "gossip the gospel," as one of the elders at my church, Mack Stiles, likes to say.[8] The impulse to share the riches found in Jesus is a natural overflow of the love of Christ that controls us (2 Cor. 5:14). "Once we are sure that the gospel is both truth from God and riches for mankind, nobody will be able to silence us."[9] Every spiritual blessing we have in Christ was designed to be enjoyed forever and shared as long as we live.

God Shows Satan How It's Gonna Be

Paul said that God appointed him to preach the mystery of the panethnic church. And then he gave a reason for this church's existence: "so that through the church the manifold wisdom of God might now be made known to the rulers and authorities in the heavenly places" (Eph. 3:10). We need to know that Satan & Co. didn't look at Adam & Co. and protest, "What *on earth* is God doing?" No, Satan & Co. look at Last Adam & Co. in utter dismay. Lo, their doom is sure. The evil powers and principalities respond with such dismay because it's utterly embarrassing. Satan successfully tempted Adam and Eve to sin, setting up the fall of the entire race of God's image bearers into spiritual zombies (Eph. 2:1). Satan successfully twisted the order of the home God created for us, ruling it with "the course of this world"

(Eph. 2:2). But God. *The audacity.* "For God so loved the world, that he gave his only Son, that whoever believes in him should not perish but have eternal life" (John 3:16). Take that, Satan.

I've tried to think of ways to express this concept of divine vindication and vengeance in ways that my elementary-aged children can understand. The best phrase I can come up with is that "the existence of the church is God's cosmic *booyah* to the Devil." But really, even that terminology is too benign for what God is really doing to Satan and his demons as Jesus builds his panethnic church. Author Tony Reinke describes the dramatic nature of what is happening through the building of the church in this way:

> What stands out in Ephesians are the ways in which the defeat of the evil "powers and principalities" is made manifest. To put it bluntly, the multi-ethnic church, living in unity, is a cosmic middle finger to the powers who have tried to force division and enmity among humanity. So now, where the New Creation people of God clash with the "powers and principalities" is the place where the redeemed on earth prove to have broken through the cosmic evil. This is not a mere marveling, but a confounding, a place of divine confrontation with evil, whereby the victory of Christ is manifested to the universe, in the local church.[10]

Reinke's words remind us that the big picture includes things we can't see. Sadly, our understanding tends to be rather limited in scope and grounded in things we can see. The universe is the cosmic stage for the glory of Jesus, and the church is the leading lady. There isn't a community in the world like her. The Son of God became incarnate, allowed himself to be unjustly crucified, victoriously rose from the dead, and is now currently cleansing, nourishing, and keeping for himself a bride. The curtain remains open on the church so that the evil principalities can tremble as they see how the gospel of Jesus Christ turns spiritual zombies into a unity-loving, harmony-seeking, cruciform church. That empty tomb in a garden was just the beginning. Christ's victory over the demonic realm is made obvious as they witness the manifold (i.e., multicolored[11]) wisdom of God. Satan's hold over the hearts of the elect is broken—the sheep will hear their Shepherd's voice. Christ has bought us—men, women, and children from all nations—with his blood. Grow, church, grow!

The Geometry of Love in the Community Garden

We grow in Christ because we must—it is who he has designed us to be. But how does this happen? Are we like cut roses in a vase? Single stems in a bud vase? Neither. The gospel frees us to know the love of Christ that surpasses knowledge, and this love has a context—the garden of community. Paul prays in Ephesians 3:17–19:

> . . . so that Christ may dwell in your hearts through faith—that you, being rooted and grounded in love, may have strength to comprehend with all the saints what is the breadth and length and height and depth, and to know the love of Christ that surpasses knowledge, that you may be filled with all the fullness of God.

Rather than plucking us out of Christian community to show us Christ's knowledge-surpassing love, God plants us in the body of Christ. This is where we are "filled with all the fullness of God," which is a phrase Paul uses to describe spiritual maturity. In other words, we grow in the garden of the local church, not in a vase all by ourselves. Jesus dwells in the hearts of individuals by faith, and it is together "with all the saints" where we explore the all the geometry of Christ's love. *How wide, how long, how high, and how deep is the love of Jesus?* We were made to help each other discover the answers to these questions. In this garden of community we seek the flourishing of others. Seeds of envy, favoritism, arrogance, racism, and gossip will find no place to cast down their roots when we are all rooted and grounded in love.

But this kind of fellowship can be hard to come by. Our sin hinders us from enjoying relationships. We are suspicious of one another: *She might use my self-disclosure against me.* We are manipulative: *He has a way of making other people always bow to his desires.* We are petty: *I can't stand her; the way she talks about her kids is so annoying.* We are jealous: *He had better enjoy the boss's good graces while it lasts.* We are self-serving: *Why did I even sign up to volunteer?* We would rather compartmentalize our spiritual lives to an easy chair in the living room where no one will bother us (for at least thirty minutes) than dive headfirst into messy relationships with other broken sinners like ourselves. But the gospel is here to change all of that, starting with our heart's inclination to be bowed in on itself.

With our new hearts of flesh, we find that we are now aching to share with our brothers and sisters how eternity is pressing on us rather than being content to just go around in circles with small talk. We find new and different ways to share with each other about the geometry of Jesus's love:

Do you know how far his love pursued me?

Did you see how he has changed our friend who persisted in unbelief for so long? Let's sing together about how high his love lifts our affections!

We need to pause for a moment and consider how pro-
foundly deep the love of Jesus reaches into the unsearchable
parts of our heart.

That is the kind of fellowship with one another that we were made for. The gospel bends our ingrown heart outward. Our heart's posture becomes that of Christ's—joyfully self-sacrificing.

In this garden of community we are all seeking the flourishing of the others. We want others to see and savor Jesus and to know his love that surpasses knowledge. It becomes our chief interest and aim to help others to know Christ, removing the rocky obstacles out of the way so that their roots can find anchor and pushing aside the obscuring shade so that they can lift their faces to the light and grow. In this gospel freedom we don't build walls around ourselves, but we stay planted in the garden. We have no need for such walls because Christ's perfect love casts out our fear. "The more we see the grace of God in Christ, the spirit of fear is diminished and replaced by a spirit of love and boldness."[12] We even begin to reject such walls of pretense because they cut us off from the people we now long to know deeply and enjoy as gifts from God. When the weeds of our self-interest begin to choke out our growth, we can count on the others to point out the threat and lovingly help us to cut them out. What we know about others is also transformed in the way we use it. We are no longer bound to self-serving voyeurism through social media; instead those kinds of things become our fodder to love others through prayer, encouragement, and acts of service.

This love of Christ surpasses knowledge in many ways, and one of those ways is that it makes no sense according to the worldly scheme, which says that every man and woman must look out for themselves. "To *know* what surpasses *knowledge* is the sublime privilege of the Christian. The purpose ultimately is to be filled with God's *fullness*."[13] Though our growth can be slow, awkward, or only slightly perceptible with a time-lapse lens, we know by faith that the garden is growing in such a way that the gates of hell must retreat. We need this truth more than ever in a day when we are so strongly tempted to leave the church and strike out on our own in "a personal, private relationship with God."[14]

How does God's garden grow? It grows as he plants seeds, waters, prunes, and harvests. More and more men, women, and children are entering the kingdom as the borders of that garden gracefully spread from Jerusalem, Judea, and to the ends of the earth.

Prayers in Accordance with the Super-Superlative

John, the beloved disciple of Jesus, wrote at the end of his Gospel: "Now there are also many other things that Jesus did. Were every one of them to be written, I suppose that the world itself could not contain the books that would be written" (John 21:25). I love how this verse stokes the imagination. We read in Ephesians that Christ will fill all in all, and John surmises that the entire world cannot contain the books that might be written about Jesus. I don't think this is a flourish of flippant compliment toward the Son of God—it is inconceivable that John would have made that kind of remark about Christ.

So, then, seriously, what would all of these unwritten books say? Surely they would tell everything that John left out of his Gospel from all he witnessed. But I would contend that some of the unwritten books to which John is referring have already been and are being written. As the Spirit has descended and indwells believers, he is carrying out Jesus's work. Of course the world cannot contain the books that would be written. What glorious work the body of Christ has done in Jesus's name and through his power over the centuries!

And how could we count up all the stories—unique stories and good works that God has tailor-made for us to walk in? The sovereign Christ, who reigns over all and fills all in all through his body, the church, is working still. The books are still being written of all that he is doing in and through us in the world. There is one word that Paul uses in Ephesians 3:20 that must be expanded into three words in English. In order to help us understand God's capacity to answer prayer according to his will, Paul made up a word— *hyperekperissou*, a super-superlative. It is in accordance with God's power to do very much more than anything, either conceivable or inconceivable, that we pray. This is the power that is at work within us.

When we survey the chaos around us, we do not need to wonder, "What in the world [cosmos] is God doing?" We know he is bringing all things under the feet of Jesus, filling all in all through his body, the church. He is yet working (John 5:17). The Creator has begun a new creation in his church, and he will see it through. Look at the center stage as the drama continues to unfold, giving us in-depth character sketches he has designed for the actors. Understand that God's enemies are also watching, and they are appalled. We'll see in the second half of Ephesians that it is only by God's divine power that we can show one another his divine love in the face of his enemies. Will we ask him to do far more abundantly than all that we can ask or think?

5

Walk This Way

Growing Up into Christ

EPHESIANS 4:1–16

My daughter's second-grade teacher sent an email to the parents of her students who were born in April: "We're celebrating the April babies' birthdays all together in a few weeks. Would you like to delegate the party elements among yourselves?" The moms agreed to divvy up the juice boxes, party favors, paper plates, and cupcakes. On the designated afternoon we showed up with our birthday stuff in tow. We could tell that the children had been patiently waiting all month for this celebration. One boy who was sitting by the door tipped out of his chair when we all walked in—he was so excited. If you haven't been in a room full of eight-year-olds busting out their smoothest moves to the gummy bear song while hopped up on sugar, you are missing out on quite a spectacle. After the songs were sung and the treats enjoyed, the kids had one more hour of class in which they needed to try to pay attention. On my way out the door I couldn't help but notice the cupcake pile in the rubbish bin. Some of the students hadn't eaten their entire cupcake; they had only licked off the six ounces of frosting from the top.

It's true that cupcakes aren't truly cupcakes without the frosting. The fact of the cake necessitates the attractive, delicious garnish on top. A naked cupcake base is just a naked cupcake base. It's technically not finished—you couldn't even call it a cupcake. For the readers who are still with me and haven't made a beeline to the bakery after all this talk of cupcakes, I wonder if we could say that Christian doctrine and right living are like cupcakes?

In Ephesians 1–3, Paul has laid down the foundation of our doctrine: God devised a plan in eternity past to sum up all things in Christ through creating and reconciling a new, panethnic humanity in Christ. The exhortations that follow in chapters 4–6 necessarily spring up out of this rich truth. They are beautiful, fitting adornments of the doctrine. Because the master builder laid a strong foundation, we know he will build a suitable structure on top of it. To put it rather simply, in light of what we know about God and his plan (chaps. 1–3), walking in this way (chaps. 4–6) is fitting worship. A life of proper worship is no mere icing on the cake, as though Christian conduct is just a bonus to right doctrine. Right living necessarily indicates the nature of the doctrine; it's not a real cupcake without the icing. (I apologize if I've ruined your appetite for the salad you had planned for lunch.)

The Body of Christ Does Not Swagger

Paul, the prisoner for the Lord, urges us to walk in a manner worthy of the calling to which we have been called (Eph. 4:1). The rest of his letter is going to spell out the implications of this, describing what a worthy walk looks like. As if we don't remember who has written this letter (we are three chapters in, after all), Paul describes himself again. He calls himself "a prisoner for the Lord." Do we know who *we* are? The apostle understands who God set him apart to be, what he is supposed to be doing while he is in prison, and who it is that sent him there. I think that all too often we find ourselves trapped someplace and wonder what on earth God was thinking. We fail to remember that God has sent us here to glorify him—chains or no chains. Paul does not see himself in mere human terms—sitting in a jail cell with an unknown earthly fate. He sees with eternity stamped on his eyeballs.

He writes with the authority of an apostle who is not messing around playing games as he suffers for his faith. The application of the doctrine he has described is at stake. So the first word of this second half of Ephesians is "urge" or "exhort," according to the Greek text. Of primary import is not Paul's temporary circumstance of being imprisoned but the purpose for which God placed him there. Chapters 1–3 disclose the truth of God's plan that was previously not known to us, and chapters 4–6 are the "therefore" of that truth. Everything Paul is about to say in the final three chapters has everything to do with the doctrine he taught in the first three chapters. What is this "calling" to which he refers in verse 1? It is, of course, that which he has described already: God predestined that we play a part in all things being summed up in his Son. Chapters 4–6 simply give us the improv guidelines for our roles.

We've been called from death to life! We are to live in light of right doctrine. Here's how we "get real" in our new reality as new creations. So, *how* do we live rightly now that we understand we've been given a role to play in Christ's filling all things? What manner of walking is worthy of this calling?

The apostle's mind first turns to our unity. With the unity of the Spirit in view, we see that maturity in Christian relationships has everything to do with the blood-bought unity that is ours in Christ. Our posture in this unity is one of driven, eager meekness. This meekness isn't wishy-washy compromise without regard to conviction but the gentleness of Christ's strength in us. Imagine the "richly blessed in Christ" community wholly bent on maintaining its unity in the bond of peace. This is so in the heavenly places, and it has implications for what we do with the physicality of our life here on the ground. Think of all that you have been given, and what it might look like to use it for the sake of eagerly fostering Christian unity in your local church. If you have time, you are to cheerfully give it to conversations that may be awkward for the sake of unity in Christ. If you have money, you are to cheerfully give it to opportunities to build up the body for the sake of unity in Christ. If you have physical strength, you are to use it to stay awake for that phone call, drive to that meeting, and lift burdens for the sake of unity in Christ. If you have been given a gift, you are to dream up creative ways to share it for the sake of unity in Christ.

I have a friend who has dropped what she was doing, on many occasions, in order to address a conflict that might be brewing in her marriage. Perhaps there was a miscommunication in an email, or an intentional nonverbal rejection passed between them. Eager to maintain unity in the bond of peace, she picks up where the awkwardness left off and says things that only new creations in Christ can say, like, "I've sinned against you. Please forgive me."

Another one of my friends is known for her gentle questions. If she hears something that could be taken in a negative way, she doesn't want to let a fog of ambiguity settle over the relationship. So she asks in all meekness, "What do you mean?" I'm personally thankful for all the opportunities she has given *me* to clarify my thinking or retract my opinions through her gentle question. Humility, gentleness, patience, and love play out on the stage and compel us to be passionately eager to maintain our unity in the person of Christ. When you are wholly bent on maintaining unity with all eagerness, there is no space for passive indifference to the plight of your brothers and sisters, however different they seem to you.

The first three chapters of Ephesians describe God's eternal purpose to bring all things together in Christ, and so it is that our unity under Christ is *the* destiny of every believer. Christian unity isn't a poetic metaphor; it's an enduring reality grounded in the fellowship of the Trinity. John Stott points to this from a persuasive angle:

> Is the unity of God inviolable? Then so is the unity of the church. The unity of the church is as indestructible as the unity of God himself. It is no more possible to split the church than it is possible to split the Godhead.[1]

The unity of the Spirit is a distinctly Christian unity, set apart from the "we are the world" unity that any nonbeliever may enjoy. If Jesus Christ had not died for sinners and risen from the dead in order to ascend to God's right hand, this radical new unity would not be ours. But Jesus has done these things, and he is seated in the position of supreme power over all things that could threaten to divide his body. Paul is not merely laying out a plan for Christ followers to have nice friendships with each other. The new humanity is in view. He is describing the one way to walk that is worthy of our calling as a new creation in Christ. Humility, gentleness, patience, and bearing with one another all typify the way new creations walk.

Walking in accordance with the gospel is the new humanity's expression of authenticity. This walk is *for real*. When our brother or sister in Christ offends us, our elder Brother enjoins us to move toward them and not away from them. When our brother or sister in Christ is socially aloof from us, the Spirit orients our hearts to be eager for unity with him or her.

Fact: Unity

It is as indisputable as the fact that the earth is round and revolves around the sun, though there were and still are some who doubt. There is only one body and one Spirit (just as you were called to the one hope that belongs to your call), one Lord, one faith, one baptism, one God and Father of all, who is over all and through all and in all. This is truth; it is a fact. Any attempt to flatten the earth to your liking or behave as the center of the universe flies in the face of reality. And so it goes that this seven-fold oneness is the reality in which you are living, moving, and having your being right now.

Flip through a high school yearbook or click around on Facebook pages hashtagged with your city's name. You'll find clubs and organizations for all manner of commonalities. Rugby clubs, Chinese dance troupes, nursing moms' communities, parents with autistic children support groups, ham radio networks, Couch-to-5K clubs, and so on. Christians enjoy the things we have in common with our non-Christian friends and relatives.

We can also appreciate our shared interests among Christian brothers and sisters. But the unity that we, the church, enjoy is not something we thought of or created for ourselves. Our unity is based on an alien unity—one that comes from outside of ourselves. It's a gift from the only Father who called us to this one hope (1:18) of unity with and in his only Son through the one Spirit.

How many churches are there? It's a good question, especially when we note the hundreds of different Christian denominations. According to Ephesians, there is one church. Though our celebrated distinctives may differ, the one church recognizes the Word of God, which teaches orthodox Christian doctrine as her one foundation. A Presbyterian from Kigali may claim she is the sister of her Anglican brother from Wales. My evangelical Filipino mailman knows that a Palestinian Christian woman who was baptized in a bathtub is his sister in Christ. She is closer to him in relations than his own flesh and blood who were raised in the same village and went to the same schools all their lives. Our unity is based on the unity of the triune God, who created us and created us anew in Christ according to the one gospel— the word of truth (Eph. 1:13). Is God one? Then he has one church. "The unity of the church is as indestructible as the unity of God himself. It is no more possible to split the church than it is possible to split the Godhead."[2]

The Church's Supernatural Source of Power

Because we are still influenced by the course of this world, we identify power with the token symbols of worldly power: money, numbers of people, political influence, and military strength. We're even tempted to confer power to churches with money, people, prestige, and might. It may be useful for a church to have a big budget to facilitate ministry and a well-networked leadership team to resource that local body, but these things are not necessary to accomplish Christ's ministry. He has his own power in mind—power that is made perfect in our weakness. "Grace was given to each one of us according to the measure of Christ's gift. Therefore it says, 'When he ascended on high he led a host of captives, and he gave gifts to men'" (Eph. 4:7–8). Read the verses in this section of Ephesians 4 and notice the ups and downs of where Christ is going. Make note of why—that he might fill all things. Now let's talk about that cloud scene from Acts 1:6–11:

> So when they had come together, they asked him, "Lord, will you at this time restore the kingdom to Israel?" He said to them, "It is not for you to know times or seasons that the Father has fixed by his own authority. But you will receive power when the Holy Spirit has come upon you, and you will be my witnesses in Jerusalem and in all Judea and Samaria, and to the end of the earth." And when he had said these things, as they were looking on, he was lifted up, and a cloud took him out of their sight. And while they were gazing into heaven as he went, behold, two men stood by them in white robes, and said, "Men of Galilee, why do you stand looking into heaven? This Jesus, who was taken up from you into heaven, will come in the same way as you saw him go into heaven."

The ascension of Christ continues as a major theme in Ephesians. In fact, it is no mere literary theme among others, but it is the grand, overarching context. We understand everything in this letter through the reality Paul is illuminating. Jesus is risen, ascended, and exalted over all things. As real or as shadowy as other circumstances in your life may feel, this is the reality that interprets all other ideas. Christ's ascension should jog our memories of God's ascension of Mount Zion after the exodus (Psalm 68). Picture Israel being led forth by God—no longer slaves, but free—and God triumphantly leading the people to the place where he would dwell. Numbers 18:6 describes how God then took for himself the Levites from among his people in order to give them back to his people to serve as priests unto him. In the last chapter of this book we saw how Isaiah 66:20–21 is being fulfilled in our midst, as God takes some men and women from every tribe and people to be "as priests and Levites." What? You don't often think of yourself as a priest or true Levite? Me neither. Our theological vision is too nearsighted, and that's why we need to remember the big story.

Remember how in the old age the Spirit was given temporarily to certain prophets, priests, and kings. Remember when King David pleaded with the Lord in his penitent prayer after his grievous sins, "Cast me not away from your presence, and take not your Holy Spirit from me" (Ps. 51:11). Understand that now, in this new age, believers in Christ are sealed with his Spirit permanently. We are in him—the last prophet, our great high priest and exalted king—and we receive gifts from his Spirit so that we, his body, might go about serving him. We have all been given different gifts to use so that we may serve as prophets, priests, and kings who build up the body of Christ, his temple on earth today.[3]

One Christ for All, and All for One Body

The victory of Christ went viral throughout the cosmos when he ascended to heaven. He plundered his enemies and rescued his own. The risen conqueror gave his Spirit to every one of his followers. Each of us was given a portion of his varied (literally, multicolored) grace. The text says that he even gave specific gifts to his church, people equipped by him to be equippers: apostles, prophets, evangelists, pastors, and teachers. Christ's perfect design for his body was that each gifted member would have deficiencies that could be met through the gifting of other members. Each member has God-ordained weaknesses that are met by the God-ordained strengths of others. He was pleased to make it so that we all need the equipping ministry of these equippers. No eye will say to any hand, "I have no need of you" (1 Cor. 12:21) in the church of the ascended Christ.

My husband, Dave, suffers from a nerve disorder that affects his arms. Over the years he has spent countless hours in physical therapy, trying to regain strength and mobility. Some of the exercises his therapists have taught him are meant to directly address the muscles in his arms. Many of the exercises, however, require a total physical response. "Every part is connected," a surgeon explained. "His arms will benefit when all the body parts are strengthened together." The doctor may as well have been reading from Ephesians 4! In verse 12 we see that all our various ministries are meant for building up the *whole* body of Christ. We don't exist for ourselves but for others. Gifts are given to us to be given to others. Gifts are for the benefit of all, not for the personal fulfillment or boasting of the gifted.

This "all for one, and one for all" ethos sounds like an idyllic neighborhood or fictional family movie. But, actually, it's more profound. What is radical about this concept is that Paul is not giving us his "best practices" tips for church growth that we may choose to implement or reject. He is describing reality, for there is not another way that the one body grows other than self-sacrificial giving. Any notion of a personal, private religion is laid to waste, for our Savior has set us apart as his public, corporate witness to his victory over the evil powers. Our dreams are subject to God, not the other way around. The culturally infused narrative that says God's purpose in giving us gifts is our own fulfillment is turned on its head. This reality grates against our quest for the holy grail of independence and proclivity for socially disengaged spirituality. And isn't that a relief?

We grow weary of watching spiritual-gift exhibitionism. The envy we feel over the gifts of others leaves a sour aftertaste. And for good reason! That way of walking isn't Christian. Such strutting is the renegade influence of the powers over the church. Our boasting sounds like a clanging gong in our own ears and the world's. It's no wonder, because such attitudes don't belong among new creations energized by the Holy Spirit. "To each is given the manifestation of the Spirit for the common good. . . . All these are empowered by one and the same Spirit, who apportions to each one individually as he wills" (1 Cor. 12:7, 11). The measuring and distributing of grace is done by the ascended one. Jesus gave gifts and grace to his one body for the sake of our growth and unity; gifts are not meant for tearing down and dividing.

When we fail to use our gifts, then, it makes sense that the body weakens. Members feel isolated and uncared for. Choosing selfishness over using our gifts is tragic because we incur needless suffering, upon both ourselves and others. A wealth of spiritual blessings and supernatural abilities and resources and strength is available to us in Christ. For the good of the body, we must embrace our God-given priestly position in the daily scattered and weekly gathered temple, using the gifts Jesus gave us. For the good of the world apart from Christ, we must live out our revelatory position as the Spirit testifies to Christ through us. All these gifts and abilities—prophecy, teaching, mercy, evangelism, and more—they're not for stashing in the closet in hopes of regifting to someone else. Any false notion that our God-given giftedness is in conflict with our God-given circumstances is set aright. Jesus, who knows better than you and I, divinely distributed gifts in such a way that would bring him maximum glory as he causes the biggest spectacle in the cosmos. We use our spiritual gifts by the strength that Christ provides so that he receives the glory (1 Pet. 4:10–11).

"Truthing" with Each Other in Rooted Love

Sometimes we think that loving others means we must pillow them in duct tape so they don't feel the sharp edges of life in this world. We might tell white lies, avoid certain people we disagree with, gloss over issues, and try to ignore the elephant in the room. All of this is done so that we may enjoy temporary, shallow comfort in our relationships. But, of course, we are people of truth, so we would never affirm that obscuring "the truth" is loving. Far be it from us to ever lie about *the* truth! When we come to Bible passages such as Ephesians 4:15, it feels kinda nice:

> Rather, speaking the truth in love, we are to grow up in every way into him who is the head, into Christ.

After all, who wants to speak the truth to someone in severity or harshness? Surely not we nice people. But the "truth" that Jane's skirt doesn't flatter her figure or that John hurt our feelings more than we care to admit is not the truth in view here. The Word made flesh, Jesus Christ, designed his body to build his body, so it makes sense that his body is nourished exclusively with his Word. "Speaking the truth in love" has less to do with gently correcting the lies someone else lives out and everything to do with building up someone else with good doctrine in a loving manner. Solid doctrine is our building material, love is our disposition, and maturity in Christ is our aim. Look at the context: Christ equipped his body with various equippers (Eph. 4:11), who are building up all of us in his Word of truth. There are specific equippers, plus we've *all* been tasked as builders who build with truth.

It is this "truthing" we do with each other, and it's what causes us to grow up into Christ. It's the way Jesus has designed it to be—there is no other way. Watch how tightly together the body-temple-growth-Word imagery is woven:

> Our growth into maturity in Christ is only possible by constant and ongoing exposure to the word of God through one another. . . . The temple of Christ's body and dwelling place of God grows by means of the word of God spoken by believers to one another.[4]

If you're anything like me, most of the time you really don't want to be bothered with things like this because you're an individualism zealot. Here is yet another point at which ecclesiology does not affirm our "what I do with my life is none of your business" mantra and "I gotta get some 'me time'" quest. Truthing solid doctrine with each other wars against our flesh while it strengthens our souls. If a toe gets stubbed, the whole leg smarts, and the body walks with a limp. Ephesians teaches us that the ascended, victorious Christ is creating in himself one new man of which we are a part. He has given us his Spirit, who has gifted every member. Every member, then, is a minister to every other member. Jesus himself energizes his body and the ministry accomplished by each member of that body. His gospel (Eph. 1:13) is the foundation and food for each member of that body. The crucified, risen, ascended, exalted, and reigning Christ is building his church on himself, just like he said (Matt. 16:18).

But there is one who would seek to destroy what Christ has built and is building.

Demonic Doctrine Diseases the Body of Christ

When the body's members aren't building up one another with the gospel (Eph. 1:13), their defenses are down and "immunity" is compromised. We cannot afford to be lax in our growth in the gospel. Satan is aggressive in his attempts to mislead, deceive, and divide us through the false teachers he animates. Peter warns us:

> Be sober-minded; be watchful. Your adversary the devil prowls around like a roaring lion, seeking someone to devour. (1 Pet. 5:8)

Notice what worried Paul about his church plants:

> But I am afraid that as the serpent deceived Eve by his cunning, your thoughts will be led astray from a sincere and pure devotion to Christ. (2 Cor. 11:3)

Without grounding in solid doctrine concerning who Jesus is, we will get tossed around according to whatever spiritual fad is trending. The illustration Paul gives is that we are like children tossed by waves (Eph. 4:14). Picture a little kid bobbing up and down in the ocean at the mercy of the current, and you're on the right track. Satan doesn't need to be creative in his attempts to divide asunder the members whom God has joined together. How does he do this? Spreading lies concerning the character of God is all Satan needs to do to divide us, just as he did in the garden of Eden. Think about the slither of that Serpent: (1) Simply hiss a lie into the eardrum or mind of an image bearer; (2) the lie tumbles around, causing chaos; (3) the immortal soul is carried away with self-consuming doubt, and (4) division and isolation occur as the heart turns in on itself. Satan knows that if you're busy coping with your own spiritual seasickness, then you are not busy building up those around you.

Not only do we need to be individually on guard against believing false doctrine, but we need to watch out for one another. The adversary's lies affect my brother and sister, and because they are joined to me and I to them, those lies affect me as well. I care deeply whether my sister is being carried away by winds of false doctrine through the pages of the latest chart-topping, so-called Christian book. I care deeply whether my brother is being tossed to and fro by the waves of the so-called prosperity gospel. Ephesians teaches us that each of us has a self-interest in the discernment of our brothers and sisters, because *self* actually refers to all of us—we are *one* body. The whole church must stand against the schemes of the Devil (Eph. 6:11).

For the love of Christ and his body, we stand on God's side against every wind of demonic doctrine. Remembering God's purpose to display his wisdom to the evil powers and principalities helps anchor our hearts rock steady when our flesh prefers to drift away in order to avoid confrontations with false doctrine. Think of the sick feeling you get in the pit of your stomach when you imagine a situation in which you need to confront a fellow member of your church. Some of us don't need to stretch our imagination too hard to think of examples where we've had to do this. Love compels us to anchor ourselves *and* our fellow members on the Word of truth so we are not tossed in the waves. Love compels us to study the Word of God deeply and handle it rightly so we don't sacrifice its true meaning on the altar of our culture or personal preferences.

The church is growing up in every way into Christ, expanding in him through the use of the gifts he has given us. "Look what Christ is doing," we say to the watching world, while the wisdom of God is being made known even in the heavenly places (Eph. 4:8–16; cf. 3:10). This "body building" is a spectacle of cosmic proportions. Christ fills the earth with the glory of God as he fills his church. All the cosmos is watching as the one body grows into a mature man through cheerful, consistent obedience to Christ's word of truth—the gospel. All people will know we are Christ's disciples by our love for one another (John 13:35). Rooted and grounded in such love, may our love abound more and more, with knowledge and all discernment (Eph. 3:18; Phil. 1:9).

How Does the Presence of God Increase in Us?

We are God's Word-dependent creatures, created in his image. Like little icons of Christ, we think with his mind, speak his truth, and serve like him. Remember, though, that the world hated him. Jesus said the world would hate us too (John 15:18). Those who walk in darkness do not rejoice as our light is shed on their deeds, pricking their numbed conscience. We will be persecuted for righteousness' sake (Matt. 5:10), but Christ's power will be made perfect in our weakness (2 Cor. 12:5–10). This is the case because Christ is our pattern. Humility, gentleness, patience, bearing with one another in love—going low is part of our high calling. Our living sacrifices are part of Jesus's design for his body on earth, for he sacrificed his life on the cross.

We adopt a cruciform posture of triumphal weakness, such as we see in 2 Corinthians 6. Every day around the world, Christians are maligned in newspapers, chat rooms, and board rooms. "We are treated as impostors, and yet are true" (v. 8). Followers of Christ are marginalized for their faith, passed over for business, elections, and grades—forgotten. We are "unknown, and yet well known" (v. 9). Greatly exaggerated reports circulate about the premature death of the church, as though the church was born on the wrong side of history. We are treated "as dying, and behold, we live" (v. 9). Our houses are burned, mothers torn from their nursing babies and thrown in prison, and men executed en masse. God's people are "punished, and yet not killed" (v. 9). Every believer undergoes daily trials "as sorrowful, yet always rejoicing" (v. 10). Many lack food, medicine, and shelter "as poor, yet making many rich; as having nothing, yet possessing everything" (v. 10).

Our need for Christ to conquer on our behalf includes "the many and terrible enemies arrayed against us. These include the Devil, demons, the world (viewed as a system set against God and his people), human enemies (John 13:2, 27; 2 John 7), death, and hell."[5] Are you feeling overwhelmed by the tossing waves? Sensing the tug of Satan's persuasive schemes? Remember we have a champion who has gone before us, given us his Word of truth, and distributed gifts so we can grow up into him. As we throw ourselves on Christ and refuse to compromise our witness—despite persecution from without and fleshly impulses from within—God's presence is made evident to the watching world. And the fullness of Christ's presence *grows* in us! "It is this reflection of God's glorious presence that extends out through Christians and imbues others who do not know God, so that they come to be part of this expanding temple."[6]

We think, speak, and live as though we are on our way to a better country and awaiting deliverance from another world. And so we are. If the Lord Jesus does not return before we close our eyes in death, may it be said of us:

These all died in faith, not having received the things promised, but having seen them and greeted them from afar, and having acknowledged that they were strangers and exiles on the earth. (Heb. 11:13)

A motley crew of racist, sin-sick, spiritual zombies is now one body under Christ. And individually they are new creations walking in humility, gentleness, and patience. They lean in to all the creative, Word-filled, Spirit-given gifts in order to build up one another. See how they love one another! Together, the life of Jesus is being progressively manifested in the flesh of this mortal body, the church (2 Cor. 4:11). We walk in a manner worthy of our calling—a bridal march unlike the world has ever seen.

6

Getting Real

Wake Up and Put On the New Self

EPHESIANS 4:17–5:14

The life of God touches every aspect of our being. The destiny of every Christian is to become what they are in Christ. As F. F. Bruce has said, the first half of Ephesians describes the new humanity as a divine creation and the second half as how the new humanity behaves in its earthly life.[1] Through faith in God's future grace, we press on toward our goal as we resist the course of this world.

But if our destiny is to become what we are in Christ, what does it matter what we think? Is our transformation not inevitable? What do these detailed doctrinal implications really do for us? Well, simply put, what we believe concerning doctrine determines the way we respond to God, his church, and this world, which in its present system is marked out for destruction.

Doctrine matters when you're reading the news and can't stop weeping. It matters when your neighbor tells you she's pregnant, and the next time you see her, she says, "I took care of the problem." It matters when your husband comes home from the office early with a cardboard box full of his pictures and lunch dishes from work. It matters when you're facing another evening of free time and you feel restless. It matters when your prayers are answered and a door to share your faith swings wide open. When your new medication doesn't do anything; when you get a raise; when your laptop crashes; when you are shopping at the grocery store; when your child rolls his eyes at you; when you're laughing so hard your face hurts; and when you get a phone call you never thought you'd receive. In every moment of life, doctrine matters. From the global concerns that affect everyone on this planet to the minutiae of our vaporous lives, doctrine matters.

Day in and day out, the cosmic drama unfolds. Since the dramatic redemption is carrying on, of course we want to play our part. God did not create an understudy for you; your entire life was in his mind from eternity past. And now, if you are in Christ, you're finally where you were meant to be in this age. He's placed you in the body. Such detail and care he has taken! We learned that the body of Christ grows by the Word of Christ, flexing its muscles to serve, stretching out its hands to heal, and dreaming up creative ways to bless one another using the gifts God has given. Rooted and grounded in love, we are the gathered-and-scattered sanctuary of Christ's presence on earth shining light into a dark world. We're driven by the purpose God gave us: to shine his light for all the nations to see and be transformed.[2]

The Devil is *not* in these details; these details make him shudder.

From Dead Caterpillars to Butterflies

Every afternoon when I pick up my kids from school, I enjoy a visit with my friend who is a preschool teacher. One day there was a small plastic cage full of leaves on the shelf in her classroom. A parent had filled up the container with caterpillars that had appeared on their patio and added leaves from a nearby bush. A school holiday was coming up soon, so I saw an opportunity for a temporary pet for my pet-starved children. I asked if we could be caterpillar sitters. My friend agreed and let us take the critters home. We added drops of water to the leaves every once in a while and removed chewed-up twigs. The caterpillars grew fat and slow. "Are there any cocoons yet?" my son asked a few (dozen) times a day.

Finally, a couple of caterpillars climbed to the top of the cage and wrapped themselves in silk cocoons. That's when it became apparent that we were not going to have a cage full of butterflies as we had hoped. At least twenty swollen caterpillars lay motionless at the bottom of the plastic container, half-buried in their own filth. From the way the few cocooned ones had wrapped silk around the inside of the lid, I knew that if I took the top off of the cage in order to rescue them, they might not make it. So we waited. The stink from the dead bugs wafted through the slits in the plastic lid. I avoided hovering near their cage for too long.

At last, on Easter morning (funny enough), my daughter noticed something moving inside the cage. A cocoon was twitching. Then another cocoon started twitching! I plugged my nose, held my breath, and reached in to scoop the two cocoons out of the container. Mesmerized by the wriggling cocooned creatures, my children witnessed two gorgeous, yellow swallowtail butterflies emerge out of darkness into the daylight. Their wings were wrinkled and wet at first, but as they kept moving and basking in the sunlight through the kitchen window, their wings unfolded.

Our own transformation is similar. The "image" we are conformed to in our unbelief is that of death and decay—we deliberately exchange God's glory and reflect our idols instead of God (cf. Eph. 4:17–19 with Rom. 1:18–28). Through the Spirit, we who were dead in the futility of our minds and steeped in our sin are now undergoing a metamorphosis into the image of Christ. None of this re-creation and renewal is owing to anything we have done (Eph. 2:8–9). Glutted to death on our own greed for more sin, we didn't have a fighting chance. God is the one doing the work inside of us, so he gets the credit for the beautiful display of Christlikeness that's emerging out of our once hardened, dark hearts.

The Gentiles' (and our) alienation from God was multilayered. We saw in Ephesians 2:11–22 that we were separated from Christ, alienated from his people, strangers to the covenants of promise, had no hope, and were without God in the world. We read now in Ephesians 4:17–19 that our depravity goes deeper still—futile minds, alienated from the life of God, ignorant, hard-hearted, callous, plunging headlong into sensuality, and greedy for more.

Now, by God's grace alone, we're creatures of the new creation made in the image of the ascended one. The constitution of our hearts is changed, so we renounce our former way of life. Our loyalty is reassigned, so we serve the victorious king and walk in his loving way. We are those who have heard about

Christ and were taught to put off our old self, renew our minds, and put on the new self. This transforming act is how we are conformed to the image of Christ. Notice the similarities between our passage in Ephesians and Romans 8:28–29:

> And we know that for those who love God all things work together for good, for those who are called according to his purpose. For those whom he foreknew he also predestined to be conformed to the image of his Son, in order that he might be the firstborn among many brothers.

I bet I know what you're thinking right now. You're probably wondering if your brain would explode if you tried any harder to envision yourself as conformed fully to the image of Christ, "after the likeness of God in true righteousness and holiness" (Eph. 4:24). I can barely type a phrase of this book without my finite mind wandering back to the chicken chili I ate for lunch or checking the clock so that I'm not late for today's appointment. And I think that's okay. We are finite creatures after all. But here's some wonderful news. My friend, you and I are just beginning to participate in the resurrection. We've been sealed with the Spirit for the day of redemption (Eph. 4:30)—Jesus is coming back for us whether or not we fully understand what that means. In the meantime, we get to taste our inheritance of every spiritual blessing in Christ until we find ourselves walking in the presence of God forever in a newly created cosmos.

We do want to play the part God has scripted for us. We want to walk in the good works he's prepared for us. Let's follow along this narrative and dive into some of the here-and-now particulars of what our doctrine means for the way we live.

Oh, but first, Paul wants us to make sure we *really* understand our context.

The Horrors of the Death March

We have already learned how we were dead in the trespasses and sins in which we once walked. We get the idea, right? We were *dead*. Yet once again Paul returns to this death march so we might taste the bitter futility of our former lives, which were no lives at all:

> Now this I say and testify in the Lord, that you must no longer walk as the Gentiles do, in the futility of their minds. They are darkened in their understanding, alienated from the life of God because of the ignorance that is in them, due to their hardness of heart. They have become callous and have given themselves up to sensuality, greedy to practice every kind of impurity (Eph. 4:17–19).

As if our deadness couldn't have been any deader, we learn that we were "greedy to practice every kind of impurity." Being steeped in our sins wasn't enough for us; we lusted for more of it. How did this kind of depravity come about? If you were an upstanding citizen before you came to Christ, it may be hard to picture yourself as "greedy to practice every kind of impurity." If it's a stretch for you to understand your lostness, pay close attention to how Paul takes up the verbiage of idol worship in this passage. In it we have a mirror of truth for our hearts.

You probably don't have a statue in your closet that you hang onto for good luck. But you must realize that millions of people in the world *do* keep idols in their homes. For many of us raised in the West, idol worship seems like a foreign concept. Before we had the TV show *American Idol*, the word *idol* wasn't a part of everyday vernacular. We simply don't envision ourselves exchanging the glory of God for the image of an ox that eats grass (Ps. 106:20). To be fair, many Westerners *do* understand what it means to exchange the glory of God for a man or a woman made in the image of God. The "fear of man" is a common struggle in the Western world, whereas "fear of evil spirits" tends to be more common in the East.

The Bible describes the idols we served: they "have mouths, but do not speak; eyes, but do not see" (Ps. 115:5). We had to carry them around because they were inanimate things; we cried to them for help but received none (Isa. 46:7). You and I may not have made statues, but we fawn over the image we see in the mirror and on the magazines at the checkout lane at the grocery and in those walking around us in church, on the street, and in nature. Our idolatry is simply defined as worshiping anything other than God. And idolatry was, in fact, the nature of our worship before the Spirit enlightened the eyes of our hearts (Eph. 1:18). Regardless of our upbringing, as pagans we were led astray by speechless idols that we shaped ourselves, calling out to our wood and stone creations overlaid with gold and silver, "Awake! . . . Arise!" (see Hab. 2:18–19; 1 Cor. 12:2).

Whenever (former) detective Adrian Monk was about to explain what had happened in a formerly unsolvable crime on the TV show *Monk*, he would preface it this way: "Here's what happened . . ." In that vein, here's what happened: Satan inhabited a beast, the crafty Serpent, and slid right past Adam, who failed to expel him from the garden. Adam and Eve were subdued and ruled by the crafty beast at the Tree of the Knowledge of Good and Evil (Gen. 3:4–5). "Adam's shift from trusting God to trusting the Serpent meant that he no longer reflected God's image but must have begun to mirror the Serpent's image."[3] Failing to exercise his God-given discernment at the foot of the discernment tree, Adam allowed Satan to deceive Eve with venomous lies against the creator God, their Father, and he decided to trust in the Snake's words. Satan had promised their eyes would be open to know good and evil just like God, and their eyes were opened. But humans cannot be God, try as we might to exalt ourselves over God and decide for ourselves what is right and wrong. The irony of our judgment is that in rejecting God's righteous law to establish ourselves as our own moral authority, we become futile. In our quest for understanding, our minds are blinded.

And blind is exactly where Satan wants us to stay. He works to blind our minds to keep us from seeing the light of the gospel of the glory of Christ, who is the image of God (2 Cor. 4:4). Satan knows that when we behold the glory of the Lord, we will be transformed into the same image from one degree of glory to another (2 Cor. 3:18). All the forces of evil—the course of this world and the evil powers led by the Devil—array themselves against God's image bearers and draw them deeper and deeper into the idolatry our sinful hearts desire. The Devil knows we will become what we worship,[4] so he plays to our self-centered disposition.

The judgment for our idolatry is that we would resemble our idols:

> "Keep on hearing, but do not understand;
> keep on seeing, but do not perceive."
> Make the heart of this people dull,
>   and their ears heavy,
>   and blind their eyes;
> lest they see with their eyes,
>   and hear with their ears,
> and understand with their hearts,
>   and turn and be healed. (Isa. 6:9b–10)

Our worship of self and stuff is evidence of our ignorance of God. In our failure to acknowledge God rightly—that is, to worship him in spirit and in truth—we walk the downward spiral into further darkness and futility. Apart from the grace of God, we are alienated from the life of God in every way. Isaiah 53:6 says that down and down the spiral goes as all we like sheep go astray, each of us turning to his own way.

But.

God So Loved the World

The Lord has laid on Jesus the iniquity of us all and, according to his great mercy, sent Paul to the Gentiles. His preaching and church-planting ministry were empowered by the Spirit, who opened their eyes to "turn from darkness to light and from the power of Satan to God, that they . . . receive forgiveness of sins and a place among those who are sanctified by faith in [Jesus Christ]" (Acts. 26:18).

The promised deliverer, the servant of the Lord, has come. Yahweh delights in him, he is empowered by the Spirit, and he will bring God's justice to the nations. He is gentle toward the broken and the brokenhearted. He will not stop until he is finished establishing justice on the earth. God gave this servant to us "as a covenant for the people, a light for the nations, to open the eyes that are blind, to bring out the prisoners from the dungeon, from the prison those who sit in darkness" (Isa. 42:1–7). In order to break our chains and throw the light of day into our darkened minds, he had to bear away our sin. So, for our sake, God "made him to be sin who knew no sin, so that in him we might become the righteousness of God" (2 Cor. 5:21). It would not have been enough to simply wipe our foolish minds of our pagan thoughts or forgive our past sins. Our callous hearts had to be replaced by hearts of flesh.

No longer doomed to our greediness to practice every kind

of impurity, we now long to walk in paths of righteousness for his name's sake. Our heart recoils at the thought of walking in the counsel of the wicked, standing in the way of sinners, and sitting in the seat of scoffers. Our new delight is in the law of the Lord, and even though we succumb to temptation otherwise, we *want* to meditate on God's Word day and night (Ps. 1:1–2). We long to choose life, that we and our children might live, loving the Lord, obeying his voice, and holding fast to him (Deut. 30:19–20). When we see before us the way of life and the way of death, we're inclined to choose the only way to live (Jer. 21:8). Hearts of flesh bring with them new affections and desires that can come only from the Lord. For those of us who are often discouraged by our lack of faithfulness to follow through on these new affections, we take comfort in knowing that we wouldn't have those holy longings unless the Lord had shown us grace in the first place.

Beloved, we are his. "If anyone is in Christ, he is a new creation. The old has passed away; behold, the new has come" (2 Cor. 5:17). And *because* we are his, that is why we have abandoned our old way of living, even while we yet live in a worldly environment.[5] We do not put away our idols *so that* God will then accept us, but we put away our idols *because* God has accepted us in Christ. God's transforming love for us reaches every aspect of our formerly pagan mind-set. Our new-creation minds have been given understanding of spiritual things. The Spirit empowers us to use our reasoning in accordance with God's Word. We can think properly along the lines of Scripture's intended meaning. Our decisions can be lined up with God's will. No longer unable to understand the gospel, we now embrace the gospel and see that it is God's power unto salvation.

All this grace is owing to the generosity of the Lord Jesus, who gave his life for ours on the cross. The big blame shift happened there. We were fully responsible for refusing the light available to us. We were content in our ignorance, amusing ourselves with moral autonomy. We were content in our callousness, having lost the capacity to feel embarrassed by our idolatry. But God gave his one and only Son, who stood in our place to be the sacrifice for our immorality—our lust for things other than God. And God willed to crush his Son and put him to grief (Isa. 53:10). For our sakes.

Facebook and Instagram give us opportunities to understand varying levels of "knowing" people. There's even an acronym for the distinction between knowing someone "in real life" (IRL) and just being "online friends." In the Old Testament, to know God meant that you not only knew him in real life but that you responded to him in a close personal relationship. You didn't merely know things *about* him like you would know someone through his bio. You knew *him*. I've heard some people describe the Bible as "God's bio." I think that's only partial truth, because God's Word is God speaking. And through the Bible, we are introduced to Jesus, the Word of God made flesh. Hebrews 1:1–2 puts it this way:

> Long ago, at many times and in many ways, God spoke to our fathers by the prophets, but in these last days he has spoken to us by his Son, whom he appointed the heir of all things, through whom also he created the world.

Before we "knew Christ" our thinking was futile, leading us only to perverted conclusions about God, ourselves, and the world around us. Watch in the next verses how Paul shows us the connection between this kind of knowledge of Jesus to our spiritual vitality.

School of Christ

After he paints the shocking and deplorable picture of what our lives were like before Christ, Paul says in Ephesians 4:20–21, "But that is not the way you learned Christ!—assuming that you have heard about him and were taught in him, as the truth is in Jesus."

There is no other place in the New Testament where the phrase "learn Christ" is found, but the whole of the Bible certainly describes what that means. Christ is both the content and the teacher. He's the script and the director. The only way out of walking in darkness and indulging the depravity of our hearts is to hear about Christ from Christ. To hear his voice is to know him. To learn from him is to learn him. We understudy Jesus.

How did God deal with our ignorance so that we could learn Christ? You may not remember the hour you first believed. My hour came sometime in October of my freshman year of university. When the Spirit of God moved in my life, there were Word-filled women around me who discerned his lead. A few months in to a Bible study with a group of fellow university girls, I discovered that I was lost. We were wading through the Gospel of John, going deeper and deeper into the text. Through the text, discussions, prayer time, and sharing, the Holy Spirit rocked my boat, and I began to feel spiritually seasick. I told my Bible study leader what was on my heart. She was ready with a question for me, and she wasn't afraid of a collision: "Friend, what makes you a Christian?"

My friend (graciously) blasted through the gap in my faulty thinking, challenging my assumption that I was a believer simply because of my upbringing and culture. She was ready with answers too, re-covering the ground we all talked about in Bible study. As this younselfg woman shared with me the good news of Christ's atoning sacrifice on the cross on my behalf, by God's grace I believed it. In learning Christ I found rest for my weary soul (Matt. 11:29). His yoke is easy, though I daily need to ask his wisdom in order to play the roles he has assigned.

God ordained that we would learn Christ through the witness of others: "What then is Apollos? What is Paul? Servants through whom you believed, as the Lord assigned to each" (1 Cor. 3:5). And indeed, we *have* learned Christ through the gospel witness of others. The Father answered his Son's prayer: "I do not ask for these only, but also for those who will believe in me through their word" (John 17:20). Paul based his entire life and ministry on the assurance he received from the Word (e.g., Isa. 6:9–10) that the Gentiles were to learn Christ—to know him: "Therefore let it be known to you that this salvation of God has been sent to the Gentiles; they will listen" (Acts 28:28). The Great Shepherd came to seek his lost sheep, and his call goes out through his words in our mouths: "I have other sheep that are not of this fold. I must bring them also, and they will listen to my voice. So there will be one flock, one shepherd" (John 10:16).

We've said before that in Ephesians 4–6 Paul is describing the manner in which we are to live out (i.e., act in line with) our new identity as a corporate body of Christ and as individual members. He describes the things that no longer make sense now that we are "we" and we are in Christ. He describes the things that correspond with the fact of our new humanity in Jesus. What is a walk that is worthy of the gospel? It's us, by God's grace, living out our blood-bought identity in Jesus. In the school of Christ we are taught in him to put off our old self. That old self belongs to our former manner of life and is corrupt through deceitful desires (Eph. 4:22). Our thoughts steer the affection rudder of our hearts, and we have a need to be renewed in the spirit of our minds (Eph. 4:23).

[Paul Drops Mic. Body Walks This Way.]

Overwhelming. That is what this call to holiness feels like to the saint. It is overwhelming in many ways. (1) We long to be holy as God is holy. Our hearts agree that God's commands are in line with God's character and the nature of his new creation. (2) We fail every day. In our pagan days we had futile minds, and now that we are new creations we need to be renewing our minds according to Christ every day.[6] The Lord provides in such a way that he is the one who gets the glory for our effort in sanctification. All this is overwhelming.

There's a line in an old hymn by William Cowper that I've often turned to in prayer. It highlights the fact that we need God's help to walk in a manner worthy of our calling:

> The dearest idol I have known,
> Whate'er that idol be
> Help me to tear it from Thy throne,
> And worship only Thee.[7]

In keeping with the Spirit's holiness, we're to put on the new self, created after the likeness of God in true righteousness and holiness (Eph. 4:24). This kind of work sounds miserable at first glance, but Richard Sibbes shows the connection between our happiness and this call to right living: "The happiness of man consists in communion with God and conformity to him."[8] We happily follow the Lamb everywhere he goes, including to the dark places of our heart where he means to do his idol-tearing work. We learn Christ through thousands of daily deaths-to-self. This next section rattles loudly with the nuts and bolts of how we are to die to our sin and live to righteousness.

When I studied Ephesians 4 it became more and more obvious that this new-creation life is not about me. Again we see the body element in verse 25 as our motivation: ". . . for we are members one of another." And then later in the exhortation Paul mentions the Spirit, who is the means by which we are connected to Christ and one another: "Do not grieve the Holy Spirit of God, by whom you were sealed for the day of redemption" (v. 30). The implication is startling. Out of gratitude we walk in God's ways according to the Spirit who was given to us. Not to do so would be a hallmark of an ingrate. Remember: the Spirit of holiness stands against the Devil, the blasphemous enemy of God.

The Spirit desires that Satan would have no place for even a foothold in our midst. That's why he is grieved when our sin divides us. It grieves the Spirit when unbridled anger among members of the body gives the Devil wiggle room. Lying, stealing, abusive language, vulgar words, slander—none of these evils is a matter of personal, private sin. They are an attack on the unity of the body that Christ died to purchase.

Paul is not merely giving us a checklist of moral behaviors: Quit stealing. *Check*. Start working. *Check*. No, these ethics show an indicative reality being played out through imperatives.[9] We are to be what we are becoming. Paul is sharing the playwright's heart for the cast's new stage direction. We're still in chapter 4 and he's nowhere near finished. And neither is God. So we're overwhelmed by grace at every step.

Stage Right, Stage Left, Center Stage, or *Wherever* You Are: Walk in Love

Walking in love as Christ walked in love is a pace marked by ongoing, sacrificial giving unto the Lord. Such a walk is a fragrant offering to him. He inspires it, empowers it, and gets all the credit. Step by selfless step, our love to one another pleases God and exalts his name among the nations. God is glorified when a thief's hands become calloused by hard work so they can give. His name is exalted when a slanderous tongue lets loose in edifying words to build up others. We used to offer ourselves in worship to our idols, but now by the mercies of God we present our bodies as living sacrifices to him. And the watching cosmos is astonished.

Everything that belongs to the old self is to be cast off and discarded—sexual immorality, impurity, and covetousness (Eph. 5:3). All our filthy speech, foolish speech, and crude jokes must be replaced by thanksgiving (v. 4). The consequences for refusing to walk in love could not serve as a more severe warning than the one Paul gives in verse 5:

> For you may be sure of this, that everyone who is sexually immoral or impure, or who is covetous (that is, an idolater), has no inheritance in the kingdom of Christ and God.

If we want to be among those who inherit the kingdom of Christ, we will flee from the darkness we once lived in. Even as temptations assault us on both sides of the road, and a shroud of deception hangs in the air, we can by God's Spirit resist the gravitational pull of the course of this world and enter through the narrow gate. The only reason this is possible for us is that Christ's sacrificial death on the cross has broken our chains. Being conformed to the image of Christ means that we are no longer bound to principles that held our hearts in sway as the world carved its image on us. Do you see in the next verses our new, permanent identity as the basis for Paul's remarks about dark and light? At one time *we were* darkness, but now *we are* light in the Lord. And so it simply goes to follow that we walk as children of light and try to discern what is pleasing to him (Eph. 5:8–10).

I love that these strong exhortations to holy living and severe warnings are joined with reminders of our being sealed for redemption. The day of redemption, a phrase unique to Ephesians, directs our thoughts toward the future grace of Christ's return. God has begun his good (new-creation) work in us, and he will assuredly complete it (Phil. 1:6). Our faith to keep walking in love is strengthened when we recall our preciousness before him.

In the meantime, we need daily intervention because our steps can be drawn back into the shadows. Walking in love (as we learned about the body of Christ from the previous passages) is a community project. The dark forces that attempt to weave us back into ungodly patterns of living are constantly at work in the world. Those perverse values make up a pervasive way of life. How can an isolated Christian stand up to such pressure alone? We are all being assaulted both overtly and subtly by the darkness that opposes the light of Christ. You and I desperately need other Christians in our lives who are willing to interrupt our dark thoughts and show us the brilliant light of the Word.

I've been blessed to have many friends who are willing to reach out and grab me when I appear to be stumbling off into thoughts that are not consistent with truth. A few of my friends are rather blunt in their approach: "That's not true, Gloria." Some are gracious interrogators: "Hmm. Tell me where you get that from." And one friend in particular just has to raise a literal eyebrow in conversation, which gives me a clue that my speech is inconsistent with thanksgiving. If you have friends like this in your life, praise the Lord for them, and let them know you are putting their number in your speed dial. If you are lacking friends like this in your life, ask that the Lord would both make you this kind of friend to others and give you fellowship with others who want to walk as children of light.

The Best Part of Waking Up

Are there sleepwalkers in your life whom the Spirit is rousing awake? As they're waking up, feed them doctrine—biblical doctrine! They've been wandering the world's Dumpsters, fumbling from decrepit filth to glossy formaldehyde and back again. Christianity is no mere moral code to keep zombies out of their neighbor's garbage; it's resurrection that turns them into butterflies.

The massive gospel indicatives in chapters 1–3 are at the steering wheel, driving the caravan of imperatives in chapters 4–6. A similar passage in Colossians 3:1–4 puts it this way:

> If then you have been raised with Christ, seek the things that are above, where Christ is, seated at the right hand of God. Set your minds on things that are above, not on things that are on earth. For you have died, and your life is hidden with Christ in God. When Christ who is your life appears, then you also will appear with him in glory.

Glory. We will appear with him in glory. Don't be afraid to administer heavy doses of rich doctrine. It has "everything to do with waking up those of us who are sleepwalking the years away focused both on work and play—on stuff that passes for reality when it's actually only a poor imitation."[10] It takes a little bit for your eyes to adjust to the sunlight in the morning, but walking in the glorious light is the best part of waking up.

Sacrificial Love

The Mark of God's Family

EPHESIANS 5:15–6:9

Before you continue reading, highlight the "not . . . , but" clauses in Ephesians 5:15–18. Paul is about to delineate the two ways to live, and we want to prepare our hearts for worship of the risen Christ, who embodies the holy conduct of the new-creation life perfectly. Because Jesus has opened up for us the paths of righteousness through his own body, we as his body here on earth want to "look carefully" at our own lives out of reverence for him. One last time in this letter Paul is going to use the verb *walk* to describe the way Christ would have us live.

Mind the Gap: Not . . . , But

As we've already seen in Ephesians, the wisdom of God is demonstrated in his revelation of his eternal plan (1:8–10, 17–19; 3:10). Paul prayed that we would be wise to the once-hidden-now-revealed mystery of the church. *Walking* in God's wisdom, then, means that we search out ways to live in line with the reality that he has designed. We "mind the gap" between the world's interpretation of the way things are and ought to be in light of God's wise plan for the ages. The unwise walk as fools because they think the wide gate is just as open as the narrow one (Matt. 7:13), the dark is just as revealing as the light (Eph. 5:8), and the father of lies (John 8:44) is just as trustworthy as the truth. Walking in wisdom is walking in truth. The truth is, though, that we all have gaps in our apprehension of God's wisdom. That's why we need God to give us the Spirit of wisdom and revelation in the knowledge of him (Eph. 1:17).

As we said earlier, we also need the body of Christ to help us watch our step, lest we stumble back into futile thinking (Eph. 4:23). Compromise is just too tempting. Jesus resisted the Devil perfectly and rescued us from him eternally, but the course of this world still tries to draw us back into following Satan's plan instead of God's. Besides our external Enemy, our flesh is yet disgusted by the holiness that the indwelling Spirit loves. Because sometimes we fear man more than God, we're tempted to give each other a pass in our struggle against (or lack thereof) sin. It might create awkwardness if I try to help my sister's halting steps in the path of righteousness. I'd rather avoid communication with my brother who has turned around and started running the wrong way. I think, though, in accordance with what we've already learned about our body life, we've seen why walking in wisdom takes the whole body. Christ, our head, desires this for us and empowers our struggle against sin until we enter his final rest.

In my husband's sermons in which he takes up the topic of church discipline, he consistently exhorts the congregation to watch his life for sin and to hold him accountable for it. He says things like, "I need church discipline because I want to be holy as God is holy. Please, *please*, don't let my sin slide by. I need you all to care for my soul!" In a way that rings soundly with echoes of grace, we are our brothers' and sisters' "keeper." To intentionally place oneself under the watching eyes of others for the purpose of growing in holiness is wisdom that can come only from God himself.

We want and need to walk this way because it falls under God's plan for the entire cosmos. Being careful how we live includes knowing what his will is. We don't want to live cosmically out of sync. Such a condition would be undeniably painful and confusing, part of the zombie culture of death in which we once walked. Zombie life is no life at all, and the demonic powers that once held us in darkness are yet raging. That's why we snatch up every opportunity we can to walk in wisdom: "The days are evil" (Eph. 5:16). We help one another along in rejecting the lies that whisper poisonous nothings of holiness-free, conflict-free coasting straight back into the arms of the Accuser of the saints. This cannot and must not be our destiny, as we have been sealed for redemption by the Spirit (Eph. 4:30) and have already begun to participate in the glorious new creation as children of light (Eph. 5:8).

When you see the argument Paul makes about drunkenness, at first glance it may seem random, but when you see the argument Paul makes, it stops you in your tracks. Drunkenness just isn't a new-creation activity. The reason he gives is that if you are filling up on wine, then you are not purposefully seeking to be filled with the Spirit. Stumbling in drunken confusion, a priest in the kingdom of Christ cannot be self-controlled and sober-minded for the sake of his or her prayers (1 Pet. 4:7). This verse is not a prohibition for Christians to never drink alcohol but an admonition to avoid drunkenness, which spawns debauchery. This is yet another way we can help one another along paths of righteousness and avoid the gap between futile thinking and God's wisdom. We who have our hope set on watching for the appearing of Jesus ought not be helplessly seeing double.

Be Filled with the Spirit

One of my children once asked me what it feels like to be filled with the Spirit: *Do you feel stuffed full like you ate too much? How do you know when you're filled up?* Those are good questions, aren't they? The Spirit-fullness we desire is not a belly-aching overdose, but worship-full expression of the life of God in us. This teaching is connected to the verses we've just gone over, as careful living includes walking as one who is filled by the Spirit. And Paul's remarks about the Spirit set up the rest of the paragraph through verse 21, in which we read about what it means to be filled with the Spirit. We are being filled with the Spirit in our Spirit-empowered speaking, singing, giving thanks, and submitting.

While we have been given the Spirit and are sealed by him, our ongoing need to be filled by the Spirit says something about the times in which we live. The kingdom of God has not yet fully come (this much is obvious), but we have already begun to taste and see our eternal fellowship with God through Christ. In Ephesians 5:1, recall how Paul urged us to be imitators of God. In order for this to happen, the Spirit must mediate the filling fullness of God to us so that we might be transformed into the likeness of Jesus. We, Christ's body, have not yet reached mature manhood (Eph. 4:13). One of the ways we know this is happening is demonstrated in the way we speak to each other and sing in both our despair and our joy unto the Lord. Such speaking and singing are among our priestly activities, a God-ordained way of strengthening our faith through the gospel. Sing like Buddy the Christmas elf, who says, "The best way to spread Christmas cheer is by singing loud for all to hear." Though I can't carry a tune in a bucket, I am encouraged that my praise to God is also a witness of his royal love to those around me.

The life of God in us is both demonstrated by and amplified in the way we communicate with others and submit to one another as we reverence Christ. We rehearse God's truth to one another as an expression of the fact that we live in the inaugurated new creation. Our words are gifts for building. The hope we have in all our conversation, writing, texting, and singing psalms-hymns-songs for one another is that it would bless the hearer or reader. We don't live to hear them say thank you *to us*, but we aim for our communication to inspire their gratitude *toward God himself*. We bless others with our words, not for them to sing our praises, but so their hearts would make melody *to the Lord*:

> Let the word of Christ dwell in you richly, teaching and admonishing one another in all wisdom, singing psalms and hymns and spiritual songs, with thankfulness in your hearts to God. (Col. 3:16)

No, we're not looking to be stuffed full of the Spirit like a plush Build-a-Bear getting stuffed once and for all in the store before an eager child takes it home to play. As we let the word of Christ—the truth of the gospel—dwell in us richly, Christ will fill us by his Spirit with the fullness of God.

May God grant us grace to not short-circuit that filling by grieving the Holy Spirit: let's be personally involved—as individual new creations and as a corporate new humanity—in subjecting ourselves to God's growth plan for us. His Spirit is growing us up into Christ our head, changing us to be more and more like Jesus.[1] Let's now look to see how this happens as we submit to one another according to the design God has given us in our relationships with one another.

Voluntary Submission to Other Sinners by Grace through Faith in Christ

Another way the Spirit-filled believer acts in line with God's will is by "submitting to one another out of reverence for Christ" (Eph. 5:21). It makes sense that submission to other sinners out of fear of Christ is a Spirit-empowered feat. It has to be. No sooner do we hear an exhortation to submission than we hear in our minds all the exceptions we want or need to make. Since this is the case as we continue to live in our fallen world, we would do well to let our hearts fly immediately to thoughts of Christ, who never abuses, flaunts, or manipulates his rightful, perfectly executed authority and rule. We submit happily and voluntarily to our perfectly good and just King, who does all things well. All our submission is to be done unto Christ.

We take Ephesians 5:21 as a general heading about what Paul is set to describe in specific detail, applying a particular submission to several different kinds of relationships in the Christian family. The German Reformer Martin Luther called this "code" a *haustafel* (literally, "house table"). We need to pay close attention to the *semantic* scope of the verb *submit* in this verse, for Paul is not calling all Christians to put themselves under the authority of every other Christian. Of course, we body members respond to other members with deferential treatment and mutual courtesy, but the submission here in Ephesians 5 is different. It is an ordered relationship in which one person is in authority and another person under authority. Some have misunderstood verse 21 to refer to husbands and wives, but as I just mentioned, this verb is a general heading for the household code Paul is about to describe (Greek scholars note that there is no verb in verse 22).

Gentle reader, we make no mistake: our submission to those in authority over us is a work of grace. It is fruit that is part and parcel of Christ's coming kingdom—a good work foreordained by God that we are now walking in (Eph. 2:10). There is no way that wives can submit to husbands, children to parents, and servants to masters if they are not being filled by the Spirit. Spiritless submission is what Paul calls insincere "eye-service" (Eph. 6:6; Col. 3:22). It's a rolling of the eyes rather than a faith-full gaze fixed on Christ our Lord in all our voluntary submission. But with our enlightened hearts spellbound on our Bridegroom, we look to him for the glorious grace he has promised.

Christ's Subversive Code

In ancient Graeco-Roman culture the normative household codes were associated with the government and politics, with an eye toward practicality. For example, if you treated servants well, they would be productive, and the nation would benefit. The emphasis was on the people under authority, laying down their code of conduct. Christ's people, however, serve the King, who fulfilled the "law of love," keeping every one of his Father's commands on our behalf, and gave us a new heart and his Spirit so that we could follow him.

> If you love me, you will keep my commandments. (John 14:15)

> Owe no one anything, except to love each other, for the one who loves another has fulfilled the law. (Rom. 13:8)

> For the whole law is fulfilled in one word: "You shall love your neighbor as yourself." (Gal. 5:14)

Christian household codes are modeled after Christ, by whose power we live accordingly. Unlike secular household codes, where those *under* authority are addressed, in Christ's household those *over* others in authority are also instructed. This is radically subversive in view of the evil powers that hold the course of this world in sway, where the strong, manipulative, and abusive inherit the earth. Husbands, parents, and masters must live according to the obligations upon them as well. Earthly productivity and efficiency are not so much in view here, as are the sovereignty and justice of God: the Creator is not partial to those he has placed in authority, but all are accountable to him (Eph. 6:9). The commands to love and to submit must remain together and interpret one another.

The law of love is to be observed and adored and its benefits enjoyed by all in and under authority. Through his people's obedience to his lordship over every area of their lives, Christ is demonstrating to the evil powers that he is bringing all things together in himself (Eph. 1:9–10). That is how a wife's submission to her husband is unto Christ, a child's submission to his parents is unto Christ, and a servant's submission to his master is unto Christ.

Jesus is about his business of redeeming all things and making all things new—from the way a wife trusts her husband's leadership, to the way a husband lays down his comfort for the sake of his wife; from the way a believing child relinquishes her opinion to follow mom and dad, to the way parents choose to be gentle and patient toward their kids instead of rude and exasperating; from the way a worker honors his boss at work, to the way supervisors generously give their employees everything they need plus more. These acts of submission are not for the sake of mere efficiency in light of the motherland, but they are the tiny mustard seeds of Christ's kingdom, which is growing as its branches spread throughout the whole earth.

A Wife's Free Submission to Her Husband

All this talk of the new humanity sounds odd to the modern ear, I know. But if we go back to the creation narrative, we find strength for our faith and clarity for our role in this cosmic drama. I think wives will be particularly encouraged by this as they consider their submission in fear of Christ. Of course, we understand that Jesus came up out of the ground on the third day into resurrection life according to the Scriptures. As Jesus created the seed for every plant after its kind on the third day, the seed for this new humanity was always in him, the last Adam. And when he, the firstfruits from the grave (1 Cor. 15:20), came up out of the ground on the third day, his resurrection ushered in this new age into which we have been placed. We no longer have to bear fruit in keeping with death. We are in Christ, our living head, through whom we bear fruit in keeping with repentance and righteousness. It is in *this* age of Spirit-empowered obedience to Christ that we are living out our roles. We have *every* reason to believe that God is for us in our *every* effort to look carefully how we walk in accordance with his wisdom and understanding his will (Eph. 5:15, 17).

Jesus effectively rescued his church out of the domain of

darkness and placed us into his kingdom of light. The Accuser of the saints is still raging about this. Yet the fact remains: we (Jew, Gentile, husband, wife, child, parent, servant, master) have each (equally) been sealed for redemption. Our radical oneness with Christ and subsequently with one another is the heartbeat of the Ephesian drama. This household code, therefore, *in no way* repeals or contradicts our unity in Christ and equality in his kingdom. The Bible's eschatological vision for the new humanity in Christ is the only place we see equality in its truest form. Just to reiterate this fact: there is no inferiority among the members of Christ's body—Jew or Gentile, husband or wife, child or parent, servant or master. Because we are the new humanity, even though our roles are not equal *in sameness*, our submission to Christ's order for the Christian household is actually an expression of our equality of dignity and personhood.

The Spirit-filled wife is joined to Christ in the new humanity he has created in himself. He has torn down all barriers of inequality among his people. The Christian wife is free in her voluntary submission to her husband, just as the Spirit-filled church is free in her voluntary submission to Christ. We must make note of what Paul is *not* saying. He is not saying that every woman submits to every man, but wives submit voluntarily to their own husbands. A Christlike husband would never and must never constrain his wife to submit to him. The voluntary and free submission of a wife to her husband is a picture of the church's submission to Christ. That is why a wife's submission to her husband is no servile condescension of her personhood, but it is worship as unto the Lord Jesus, who never denigrates or demeans his bride, the church.

And so it is, the wife is like Christ in her humble obedience to the Father as she submits to her husband "in everything," that is, in all the areas of her life. That wives should be subject to their own husbands "in everything" is not a reference to comprehensive obedience but to every sphere of her life. Of course, under no circumstances should a wife submit to her husband's leadership into sin against the Lord. That would be the antithesis of submitting "out of reverence for Christ" (Eph. 5:21). Note that Paul also teaches that husbands and wives have *mutual* authority over each other's body, specifically regarding their sexual relationship (1 Cor. 7:1–5). Now we will see how the husband is like Christ in his humble obedience to the Father as he sacrifices for his wife.

The Groom Who Dies for His Bride

Outward-focused, others-centered, and Spirit-empowered, the Ephesian theme of love is what governs all our relationships. Paul gets graphic with husbands in his charge to them to love their wives. Specifically, the love a husband should show to his wife is a voluntary, glad-hearted, joy-infused initiative to be bruised, beaten, scorned, and crucified. For that, Paul says, is how Christ loved his church. Though the authority of the husband is grounded in the creation narrative (Gen. 2:24), the exercise of such authority is demonstrated by Christ on the cross. We see no such injunction to husbands: "Rule! Dominate! Conquer!" in their marriage. Instead, we see the exhortation: "Give! Sacrifice! Die!" (Eph. 5:25–28, 33). In verse 28, Paul hearkens back to the neighborly love of Leviticus 19:18, "You shall love your neighbor as yourself: I am the LORD." Husbands are to love their closest neighbor—their wife—as they love themselves. This is no sad-faced, reluctant duty. It's a win-win: "He who loves his wife loves himself" (Eph. 5:28b). In the gospel we learn that the Lord himself became our closest neighbor when he became incarnate, wearing our own flesh and blood. For the joy set before him, he endured the cross (Heb. 12:2), and in doing so he loved us to the end (John 13:1). Jesus loves his bride, who is his own body, as he loves himself. Win-win.

When I was in language school, our instructors taught using a method called "Total Physical Response" or "TPR." In order to learn a word or phrase, we needed to act it out. We did not simply look at a picture of a pencil and say "qalami" (my pencil); we were to take a pencil in our hands and affirm it through our actions and words. Love is like the TPR method of learning a new language. We may say we love like Jesus loves, but we must live it out in his strength. Like Christian wives, Christian husbands look to Christ for everything they need. They understand that the reason they love Jesus is that he loved them first (1 John 4:19). With their hearts set free by the security of Christ's everlasting love, husbands can reach out to their wives to do whatever it is they need to do by the grace of God in order to maintain unity in their marriage, because this is what Christ does for his church. Enter the living room with a smile to assuage a wife after an awkward interaction. Initiate reconciliation after an argument. Serve humbly without an eye for recompense. Lead without lording over. And give, give, and give some more.

Even though we live together as pilgrims in a post-fall world, our unity speaks of the unashamed freedom of Eden's paradise. Marriage is no social construct to merely relieve loneliness, make more humans, or share burdens (though marriage enables those things). Marriage tells a story, showing the world what Jesus is like in his marriage to the church. But even in this church age not all people are called to marriage (1 Cor. 7:1–40). Single Christians are no less cherished by Christ and should be no less valued by the churches of which they are a member. All believers, single or married, are betrothed to Christ our Bridegroom and will be arrayed in splendor at the marriage supper of the Lamb. Being found in him is our "happily ever after"—the eternal reality that even the best earthly marriage can only imitate in part. The last Adam of the new creation loves his bride with a sacrificial love: he would rather die than live forever without us. And indeed he did die. Single or married, our hearts are safe with our Bridegroom, who says in no uncertain words: "I hate divorce" (see Mal. 2:16).

Until our Bridegroom returns, we walk wisely in our earthly marriages. We know his will because he made it known to us, that is, his plan for the fullness of time to unite all things in Christ (Eph. 1:9–10). The summary of the age is coming, when the picture God is drawing is shown forth in Technicolor splendor. Brilliant as a city of gold gleaming in white light, the redeemed panethnic bride is made ready for her husband. Today and each day until that day, each husband is to love his wife as himself, and each wife is to respect her husband (Eph. 5:33). To walk this way is a joy of truly cosmic proportions.

Wait—Another Mystery, Paul?

If you are married, then you have probably heard it said that "marriage isn't all about you." Maybe your lips were the ones chiding your spouse with this phrase, or vice versa. I sometimes wonder how sinless and perfect Adam and Eve processed that truth together when God gave them to each other in marriage in the garden of Eden. Was it an obvious reality that they both simultaneously recognized? Or did it dawn on them one at a time in aha moments? Either way it went, we see something now with clarity that Old Testament personalities could see only in shadow. Adam and Eve's marriage was created to tell a story—a parable, if you will—of a certain prince and his bride.

This bride was ashamed, because, you see, she lived in futility brought on by her own sin. Her idol lovers abused and abandoned her, leaving her for dead. But. Her maker is her husband. He is the Lord of hosts, who commands legions of angels to guard her. He is the Holy One of Israel, her Redeemer who has paid the price at the cost of his own life. The prince is none other than the God of the whole earth. And he is calling her even now. Even now while she is still a sinner, deserted and grieved in spirit, he is calling her *because he has called her* (Isa. 54:1–6). She's not forsaken or desolate anymore. Her prince has given her a new name: My Delight Is in Her. Every nation will one day marvel at her radiant beauty. Moreover, her prince rejoices over her as the bridegroom rejoices over his bride (Isa. 62:2–5). She is *the* bride, the wife of the Lamb, prepared for her husband (Rev. 21:2, 9–10; 19:7–8).

Do you wonder what the people thought when Jesus claimed that he was *the* prophesied Bridegroom (Mark 2:18–20; John 3:29)? He was no imposter groom, presenting himself to the bride betrothed to Yahweh. Christ is the ultimate, eschatological "man/Adam," and the church is the ultimate, eschatological bride.[2] Now in Ephesians 5:31 Paul quotes Genesis 2:24: "Therefore a man shall leave his father and mother and hold fast to his wife, and the two shall become one flesh."

So, why has Paul brought up Adam and Eve's marriage in this exhortation for us in our marriages? Is it simply because we need a pattern to follow? Paul uses this pre-fall text to explain that marriage is between a man and a woman and is actually both pattern *and* purpose. The purpose of Adam and Eve's marriage is the same as that of our marriages today: to point to the unity of Jesus and his bride, the church.

Our shadowy marriages of earthly temporality have a purpose, according to a pattern, in order to point to ultimate reality. That reality is the rock-steady, royally loving, eternally loyal relationship of Christ to his bride, the church. That's what the mystery is about: Christ's people united with him forever until never do they part. Someday, when all the church is gathered in and Christ returns, we won't need this pointer anymore. Truly, our marriages are momentary.[3] We get to participate in the leaving-and-cleaving mystery in full view of the cosmos. Our marriages play out the parable of Christ's love for his people until he returns to take his bride to the place he is preparing for her.

Love as Serious as a Heart Attack

So what is a church to do when troubles—both great and small—arise in our marriages? To say, "Take it seriously," doesn't quite do justice to the marital mystery of human marriage and Christ's relationship to his church. What should we remember as we approach conflict within a marriage covenant? I like the way this reminder puts it:

> When problems arise in the marriage relationship, husbands and wives need to remember that there is an ultimate redemptive-historical purpose for marriage that transcends their own human relationship.[4]

Paul has just spent five chapters describing how Jesus has united a fragmented humanity in himself, is mending our broken relationships, and is continuing to fill all things by his Spirit through his church. "Serious as a heart attack" is a simile that is pretty close to the level of importance of the things we're talking about. Sinful yet redeemed men and women do not simply drift into harmonious unity and new-creation peace pursuing. Just watch a loving married couple make a decision about who gets to eat the last piece of Oreo cheesecake (or maybe just watch the married couple of which I am a part).

Sometimes "until death do us part" seems like an easier commitment to keep than sitting together at the table and planning the year's budget. Continuing to become one while eager to maintain the unity of the Spirit is a spiritual battle. Married couples need to remember to walk by faith—according to *God's* wisdom. The covenant they made is meant to reflect a "deeper magic" than mere ceremonial sayings.

> Set me as a seal upon your heart,
>   as a seal upon your arm,
> for love is strong as death,
>   jealousy is fierce as the grave.
> Its flashes are flashes of fire,
>   the very flame of the LORD. (Song 8:6)

Such awe-full loyalty speaks of Christ's love for his church, the bride for whom he pursued death in order to save. No division, including anything that can happen to us in life or death, can ever separate us from his love (Rom. 8:35). *Ever.*

Adam slept a deathlike sleep while God set apart one of his ribs and took it out of him in order to fashion for him a bride. Christ's side was opened at the cross and his atoning blood and cleansing water were poured out. He "slept" in death so that the church could be formed[5]—his bride, who would share in his resurrected life as resurrected flesh of his resurrected flesh. What God has joined together through the death of Christ—that is, in his joining together of Jew and Gentile in the church—no demon can tear asunder. And whatever married couple God has joined together from two into one flesh, let not man or woman separate.[6] We are actors on the cosmic stage, playing out the profound mystery in front of a watching world.

Obeying Your Parents in the Lord Requires Childlike Faith

Spirit-filled living and wise walking is not just for the mature of body. Children are also addressed in Paul's exhortation to Christian families. We follow the same context for their injunction as well: this is what it looks like for children to walk wisely, to be filled with the Spirit, and to exhibit their fear of Christ. Even the smallest little actors and actresses have a role to play in the cosmic narrative.

I think it is wonderful that children are given both a simple affirmation that every child can understand ("for this is right") and a reminder of God's promise to bless them as an encouragement in their role:

> Children, obey your parents in the Lord, for this is right. "Honor your father and mother" (this is the first commandment with a promise), "that it may go well with you and that you may live long in the land." (Eph. 6:1–3)

When believing children submit to their parents, they are also part of the summing up of all things in Christ. The Father is certainly pleased with the work his Son is doing in those children's lives in conforming them to look more like himself. Earthly fathers, likewise, should regard their children as God does: with deep pleasure. Specifically, what this does *not* look like is provoking their children to anger. (Parents, I think you and I know it is not hard to discern when we are sinning in this way.) Even in his discipline of the children whom he created, redeemed, and cares for, the Father's heart toward us is *love* (Heb. 12:6; Rev. 3:19).

The goal in our parenting is not rote obedience but that all of our discipline and instruction would point our children to the Lord, because it is "of the Lord" (Eph. 6:4). Both subordinate children and fathers in authority need to understand the Lord's will (Eph. 5:17). So the fruits of the Spirit mark the way we treat our children, who are the youngest and most helpless neighbors among us. Fathers (and mothers) love their children as God the Father of all (Eph. 4:6) loves his children.

Slavery, Sincerity, and Christ's Supremacy

Our household code is also an address to slaves and masters, who are both accountable to God for the way they live. It is important to note right away that when talking about masters and slaves, Paul is not making comments or judgments on the social customs of the day. This passage in Ephesians (and the corresponding one in Colossians 3:22–25) is written to the church concerning every believer's freedom in Christ (whether slave or free). Paul's instructions in this passage to Christian slaves concerned the manner in which they should serve (cf. 1 Cor. 7:21–24). In these passages we find no rallying cry for abolishing the custom of the day or justification for the obscene disgrace of modern-day slavery.[7] We know, however, from Paul's letter to Philemon the specific ways that his gospel undermined the evil of slavery in that day. The gospel undermines and repudiates the deplorable institution of slavery today as well.

Addressed here in this specific passage in Ephesians are both the manner of service and the manifestation of hope for Christians who are indentured slaves. They are to work like this: "as you would Christ" (v. 5b), "[not] as people-pleasers" (v. 6a), "as bondservants of Christ" (v. 6b), and "as to the Lord" (v. 7). The sincerity of their service unto Christ flows out of a heart changed by God and indwelt by the Spirit. Though they were indentured servants of other people, their master is Christ alone, and he alone rules their lives. Regardless of who your employer is, which country issued your visa, or who issues your paycheck, it is Jesus whom you are serving.

All things are still being summed up in Jesus Christ, and it is the Lord himself we are serving. He, the judge of all the universe, instructed slaves to obey their earthly masters with fear and trembling "as bondservants of Christ." Jesus was not threatened by the honor a slave would give to his master, as he was the one whom the slave was serving. Our Good Shepherd was also not the one being confounded as one of his beloved sheep was found in the employment of an earthly master, for he himself is the sovereign Lord. He is not partial to masters or to slaves, so masters are not off the hook in their holy conduct toward those in their employment. God himself would bless, provide, and repay, and we have seen already in Ephesians the manner in which he lavishes the riches of his grace (Eph. 1:8).

Sticking It to the God of the Age

Again and again the evil powers are confounded by the startling character of the church. She is no longer walking according to the course of the world, which is animated by demonic forces. She is walking in wisdom, making the best use of the time, because the days are evil. Futile thinking is a thing of the past now, as her foolish, darkened heart has been replaced. Pouring out of her new heart is thanksgiving to God for everything in the name of the Lord Jesus Christ.

That name—the name that "boils the blood" of the Accuser of the saints: *the Lord Jesus Christ.* Now the bride submits out of reverence for Christ in accordance with his subversive code instead of submitting to Satan's perverse household code. Husbands die for their wives, though they may be ungrateful. Wives respect their husbands, though they are flawed. Parents train up their children in the Lord, though they themselves are also being trained by him. Children obey their parents in the Lord, though their moms and dads execute their leadership poorly at times. Masters and slaves together do the will of God from the heart—no more threats and no more insincere eye-service.

In this chapter we've watched how the bride walks in God's wisdom because she knows what God has planned for the summing up of all things in Christ. There is no waffling in her commitment to do so because she knows nothing will separate her from the love of her Groom. No cold feet. No jitters. And no wavering in her joy-full confidence in her Groom. Now, watch her stand. While she waits for her Groom to return and bring her to the wedding feast, her Groom has left her something to wear as she stands against the schemes of the Devil. It's not your typical engagement wardrobe, but maybe it should be. Let's look now at the armor of God.

Cruciform Armor

The Church's Subversive Spiritual Warfare

EPHESIANS 6:10–24

Finally, we've come to the conclusion of Paul's letter. It is his conclusion not only because it is at the end, but precisely because his flow of thought brings him here. "Finally," the apostle says. The flow of his arguments, the direction of his prayers, and the various exhortations all point to the fact that something unseen is happening that is more real than we can imagine. By faith we are saved through grace, and that is exactly how we will persevere to the very end of this war.

What you are about to read in Ephesians 6:10–24 is not some weird hallucination dreamed up by a prisoner in chains but the doctrinally driven application of *everything* we've read in Ephesians. Every one of us has a vested interest in owning this passage for ourselves, as we all find ourselves in the war between good and evil.

If we're all in the war, then we all need God's armor. Deep in our heart we know it's true; we feel that already–not yet tension. Jesus has *already* ascended far above all rule and authority and power and dominion (Eph. 1:21). God has *already* made us alive together with Christ and raised us up with him and seated us with him in the heavenly places in Christ Jesus (Eph. 2:5–6). But Jesus has *not yet* finished building his body up to the measure of the stature of his fullness (Eph. 4:13). Yes, the body is being built up in love, but we still have a need to resist the waves and winds of doctrine, human cunning, deceitful schemes, and the Accuser of the saints.

How do *you*, dear reader, resist this evil day? Believe it or not, here in the desert where I live, most people dress in layers to protect themselves from the sun's deadly heat. Yes, that is a very sweaty business, but it can save your life. Desert dwellers know that it's not enough to just have layers, because the wrong layer could mean suffocation for your skin (a big mistake in the desert)! The right covering makes all the difference. Same goes for spiritual protection against the schemes of the Devil.

Finally, Be Strong in the Lord

When it comes to our protection in this ongoing spiritual war, God has got us covered with what we need. What battle, you say? Why, the one being waged right now. *Arise, O sleeper!* Hopefully we do not find ourselves in the same position as King Theoden in Tolkien's *Lord of the Rings*, who recoiled at the thought of risking his army in a war. Aragorn's response to him haunts us: "Open war is upon you, whether you would risk it or not." Beloved, fellow sojourners and pilgrims, all the vile powers of evil wage war on the bride. We are corporately called into a spiritual battle against the forces of evil. The church is a bride with armor on. And her Bridegroom has clothed her in his righteousness and given her his cruciform armor to wear until he returns.

Wait—*cruciform*? Yes, we don the armor that corresponds to our new self. That new self, which is God's creation, is made in his own likeness of true righteousness and holiness (Eph. 4:24). This cruciform armor fits the bride of Christ perfectly as she was re-created so that she would suit it. God's truth, his righteousness, his gospel, and his Word—none of these things were created to suit us. No, we were the ones who needed to be re-created so that we would match the likeness of God. It is *his* armor, after all. Remember: Jesus won by dying. If the rulers of this age had understood God's plan for Christ (*and* the saints, *and* the cosmos, *and* his enemies) on the cross, then they would not have crucified the Lord of glory (see 1 Cor. 2:1–8).

Our strength comes from the Lord. Paul has already told us what the Lord's strength is like. His power is immeasurably great and it is *for* us who believe. The Lord's great might raised Jesus from the dead. Raised. From. The. Dead. It's the same power that seated Christ—the Son of Man (a human being!)—at his right hand in heaven. It's the same power he used to kill the hostility between Jew and Gentile at the cross. It's the same power that is stronger than anything we can imagine that is working inside of us (see Eph. 1:19–20; 2:16; 3:20). No, beloved, do not worry whether you will be strong enough. *God* is strong enough.

It is a passive "be strong" verb here, and to put on the new self is what it means to be strong in God's strength. We do not wrestle against flesh and blood; otherwise the body of Christ would take up butcher knives to behead our enemies. No, we wrestle against "the rulers, against the authorities, against the cosmic powers over this present darkness, against the spiritual forces of evil in the heavenly places" (Eph. 6:12). If our Enemy takes up a knife to separate our head from our body, we are not afraid because that head is coming back on at the end of this evil age. Moreover, Jesus, our head, can never be separated from his body. Our spiritual warfare takes the shape of the cross, the instrument that Jesus used to defeat the demonic powers and win over his enemies with his dying love.

The Schemes of the Devil

The deceiver of the whole world who accuses us day and night before God knows that his time is short (Rev. 12:7–12). He industriously seeks out opportunities to lure us into believing false doctrine and living in its corresponding sin. Satan disguises himself as an angel of light (2 Cor. 11:14), draws unbelievers to himself, and blinds them "to keep them from seeing the light of the gospel of the glory of Christ" (2 Cor. 4:3–4).

But our time of spiritual blindness is over. With the precision of a cataract surgeon, the Spirit removed the scales from our eyes. God caused us to turn from demonic darkness. And so we could not be recaptured again, Jesus, when he forgave our sin and placed us in his kingdom, broke the power the Devil had over us (Acts 26:18). God justified us by faith in his Son, effectively distancing us from Satan's accusations. The Devil has no claim on one placed in Christ, the last Adam, who was vindicated before heaven and earth in his resurrection from the dead. As he rose, we shall as well.

Our rescuer will keep us safe until the war is finally over.

Though we have no reason to be afraid of Satan anymore, today we are at risk of losing hope. The darkness of discouragement and distraction has a strong gravity and the doctrine of demons an enticing hook. In Paul's prayer he asked that the eyes of our hearts would be enlightened so that we could see our hope (Eph. 1:18).

Satan's accusations hold no weight, but the roaring lion still prowls around looking for opportunities to deceive God's children. We need to resist the Devil the same way Jesus did: by hiding God's Word in our hearts. Merely downloading God's Word into our purse on our mobile device just isn't near enough to help us in our moments of need.

We're Already Wearing It

As we said at the beginning of this chapter, the spiritual armor is not an aside. It is a conclusion. Careful readers will see things they've already read about in Ephesians. Paul has taken us to the armory already and shown us the spiritual weapons one by one. Now, here at the end, we have a challenge to action, a hope-filled exhortation to use them as we walk wisely. We need these things in our resistance against the personal demonic forces that are hell-bent against us. See what the Bridegroom has provided!

The word of truth, the gospel of our salvation (Eph. 1:13), encircles us. The truth is in Jesus (Eph. 4:21). It is this gospel truth about what Christ has done that we speak in love to one another (Eph. 4:15). We have every reason to be confident in the effectiveness of this gospel in our spiritual warfare. It is the power of God for salvation (Rom. 1:16). We are people who have put away falsehood and speak the truth with our neighbors (Eph. 4:25). The Enemy is repelled by the light that shines forth from our deeds of faith, because in that light is all that is good and right and true (Eph. 5:9). Christ gives us his own righteousness by faith. Into his own image—the image of God—he has re-created us to reflect God's true righteousness and holiness (Eph. 4:24). Remember whose you are. Remember who he has re-created you to be.

We've been saved by faith, which is not our own doing (Eph. 2:8). We have boldness and access with confidence through our faith in him (Eph. 3:12). Christ dwells in our hearts through faith (Eph. 3:17). We believe in one Lord and are of one faith (Eph. 4:5). Christ is about his work growing his body here on earth until we all attain to the unity of the faith (Eph. 4:13).

The divine warrior of Isaiah 59 is clothed in righteousness. And if it is covering enough for him, it is covering enough for us:

> He put on righteousness as a breastplate,
> and a helmet of salvation on his head;
> he put on garments of vengeance for clothing,
> and wrapped himself in zeal as a cloak. (Isa. 59:17)

Covered from head to toe with the breastplate of Christ's righteousness, we're also shielded by faith in the God who says, "I will never leave you nor forsake you" (see Josh. 1:5 and 2 Cor. 4:9). Father Abraham had many sons, and many sons have Father Abraham. And if we are one of them, then we have everything Abraham had by faith. Believing Gentiles and believing Jews are heirs of the promise God gave to Abraham: "Fear not . . . I am your shield; your reward shall be very great" (Gen. 15:1). The Lord covers his children with favor as with a shield (Ps. 5:12). He is a shield for all those who take refuge in him (Ps. 18:2, 30, 35).

> The LORD is my strength and my shield;
> in him my heart trusts, and I am helped;

my heart exults,
>> and with my song I give thanks to him. (Ps. 28:7)

Can you hear the Ephesian echo of thanksgiving to God and strength in his might through the lyrics of that psalm?

> Every word of God proves true;
>> he is a shield to those who take refuge in him.
>> (Prov. 30:5)

Can you hear the Ephesian drumbeat of cruciform spiritual warfare by God's Word in that proverb?

Jesus gave himself for our sins to deliver us from the present evil age, according to the will of our God and Father (Gal. 1:4). Faith in this Christ will surely shield our heart against every fiery dart that the Devil throws our way.

Jesus prayed not that we would be taken out of the world but that we would be kept from the Evil One (John 17:15). John, the beloved disciple, heard Jesus pray this prayer. And he understood by faith that God wholeheartedly agreed with Jesus's prayer and answers it through Christ affirmatively:

> We know that everyone who has been born of God does not keep on sinning, but he who was born of God protects him, and the evil one does not touch him. (1 John 5:18)

Stand like Jesus stood. Fight like Jesus fought, through sacrificial love; and be imitators of God (Eph. 5:1). "Submit yourselves therefore to God. Resist the devil, and he will flee from you" (James 4:7). We do not need newfangled strategies to resist an innovative, postmodern Satan. Christ has gone before us and shown us how his Enemy can be resisted: through the Word of God. Jesus obeyed God's Word perfectly, hiding it in his heart and throwing it back in the Devil's face every time he tried to twist it and lead Jesus astray.

He resisted to the point of shedding his own blood on behalf of the elect. Through his dying he conquered and is now standing as a Lamb slaughtered, having ransomed people from every tribe and nation and people by his blood. Christ gave his life on the cross so that while we remain between the ages, our struggle would be against *defeated* evil powers. Smile! You were once a captive, but now you've been set free by Christ. The evil powers may rule the realm of darkness, but you've been transferred on the first available flight out of this realm "to the kingdom of his beloved Son" (Col. 1:13). Even Satan's chief lackey, death, has been subjected to Christ, for through his death he destroyed the one who has the power of death (that is, the Devil). You are no longer his subject, living a slavish life marked by the fear of death (Heb. 2:14–15).

Happy Feet

I've lived in the Middle East for only eight years now, but I've been here long enough to meet some missionaries who describe coming to do ministry here as "having been dragged kicking and screaming." Sometimes they still kick and scream, dreaming of greener pastures elsewhere (and *literally* greener pastures). Ours is no reluctant call to wage spiritual warfare, for we were once captives too. Think of all the long lines of faithful gospel proclaimers who had to have donned the shoes of readiness of the gospel of peace in order to reach you.

Our feet are moved by the readiness given by the gospel of peace (Eph. 6:15). The gospel makes us quick to move toward reconciling with our enemies, repent of our ethnocentrism, honoring people in a different social class, speaking well of our authorities behind their back, sharing what little or much we have, showing appreciation for what others do for us, uniting with a local body of Christ in spirit and in truth, and dying to ourselves in every way for the sake of making Christ's name famous in all the cosmos. We rearrange our budgets, schedules, and lifestyles in order to live out the design of God in our households. We soak our minds in Scripture in order to reshape the way we think about our relationships and authorities now that we see that we are in Christ. We strategize to serve others using our gifts, we conspire with one another to serve more effectively, and we pray that the Spirit would move among us and let there be light.

Chained to Opportunities

Indeed, Paul saw that the armor we wear is truly *God's* armor, which God and his Anointed One have donned in the past and now give to elect people. Righteousness is the belt of Yahweh's waist, and faithfulness the belt of his loins (Isa. 11:5). His servant has a mouth like a sharp sword (Isa. 49:2), and he has beautiful feet that bring "good news of happiness, who publishes salvation, who says to Zion, 'Your God reigns'" (Isa. 52:7). The spiritual armor given to the church has been tested and found effective.

Equipped by the Spirit and clothed in God's armor, we enter the dark places of the world to plunder Satan's kingdom searching for captives, announcing the good news of their release.

Paul wore chains in prison and saw that they were for the glory of his readers (Eph. 3:13). Where has our captain stationed *you*? In coffee shops, school foyers, backyards, sidewalk art shows, cubicles, and grocery stores, we speak of the one who has promised true freedom. The winds of false doctrine are blowing, and the waves of trial are mounting. There is no time to waste complaining of our "chains," for we are prisoners of Christ himself. He is the one who has set us in our current circumstances, whatever they may be, for his good purpose to glorify himself. Like Paul, we see our chains as opportunities and not hindrances (Eph. 6:20).

Remember that we have every reason to be bold, for the liberty we speak of is no false freedom, like that of the false teachers who promise freedom but are themselves slaves of corruption (2 Pet. 2:19). His freedom is here now, and it is coming. Would the Spirit so fill us that we could not help but to whisper, text, speak, and proclaim that he who testifies to God's kingdom says, "Surely I am coming soon" (Rev. 22:20).

Praying at All Times in the Spirit

The bride, clad with the cruciform armor of God, is a terror to the evil principalities. She is standing firm in the strength of God, resisting the gravitational pull of the course of this world. Grace is like a centripetal force keeping us from wandering back to follow the prince of the power of the air as we formerly did (Eph. 2:2). We're no longer comfortable walking the well-worn paths of destruction. Ever gracious, the indwelling Spirit causes us to feel his grief over our sin when we lean toward the Enemy's direction. You're safe in Christ, beloved. Our captain has sealed us by his Spirit forever; there are no real "defectors" in God's kingdom. The doctrine in Ephesians teaches us that those who do return to the kingdom of darkness were never truly in the light.

She is a bride who has been saved to pray. We are safely standing in Christ even as the powers of evil assail us, and the furious dragon continues to "make war on . . . those who keep the commandments of God and hold to the testimony of Jesus"

(Rev. 12:17). Safe in Christ, we exercise our priestly privilege to pray. Do you see brokenness around you? Are you sick and tired of reading newspaper headlines that make you want to vomit? Does the sound of a ringing phone strike fear into your heart that it may be *the* phone call you've been dreading? Are there saints in your small group whose faith is failing even as the community rallies around them? Or some who have no one to help carry their burdens? Do *you* suffer? Then you are to pray at all times in the Spirit.

> As our vision is reshaped for the temple of the new heaven and new earth, we declare war on the status quo of the brokenness of this world and labor in the place of prayer in the inaugurated form of the temple. As our hearts are broken by the reality of sin in the world and injustice in society, then we must cry out before the Lord and pray.[1]

We pray to the end that we might see "the kingdom of the world . . . become the kingdom of our Lord and of his Christ" (Rev. 11:15). No government on earth can make this kind of claim. No terrorist in a cave can boast this kind of rule. No evil principality from the vilest pit of hell can feign this kind of authority. Christ *shall* reign forever and ever!

Jesus > Adam

The last Adam is better than the first Adam in every way. Adam failed to revere God's Word and execute the Serpent, who reviled God's Word. Jesus lived by every word that proceeds from the mouth of God and crushed the head of the blasphemous Serpent.

Because of his sin, Adam was subjected to toil and die in a world ruled by Satan (Gen. 3:17–19). Because of his righteousness, Jesus victoriously conquers evil and "will tread the winepress of the fury of the wrath of God the Almighty" (Rev. 19:15).

What is true of our captain is true of us. It's his breastplate of righteousness that we are wearing. It is effective and genuine. His truth holds us together. He has bound us to live in his reality—the only reality there is. It's his gospel of peace that we run about the world announcing. It is mighty to save. He himself is our shield, who covers us from head to toe. Christ our Savior is our head and our salvation—an unbreakable, uncrackable, unassailable helmet of eternal protection. The sword of the Word is his weapon for conquering. It is deadly and true. We fight like Jesus fights—loving righteousness at the cost of our lives, insisting on God's truth, spreading the good news of his kingdom, and rescuing lost people out of darkness. Our captain has been given all authority in heaven and on earth (Matt. 28:18), and it is with this authority that he has passed on these words to us:

> Go therefore and make disciples of all nations, baptizing them in the name of the Father and of the Son and of the Holy Spirit, teaching them to observe all that I have commanded you. And behold, I am with you always, to the end of the age. (Matt. 28:19–20)

Jesus came to do what Adam (we) should have done. Adam was to be fruitful and fill the earth and subdue it (Gen. 1:28). Jesus "ascended far above all the heavens, that he might fill *all things*" (Eph. 4:10). Through Adam we can be born only of blood and the will of the flesh, but Jesus causes us to be born of God, just as he was (John 1:13). Through Adam's work we are subject to death, but through Jesus's work we receive an abundance of grace and the free gift of righteousness (Rom. 5:17).

With all the enemies of God pitifully squished under Christ's pierced feet, we have nothing to fear as we go about our daily lives from here to the end of the earth, witnessing to others about what he has done (Acts 1:8). Even in the mundane moments of life, the created order has not forgotten. All creation is waiting with us with eager longing for the revealing of the sons of God, which will be the day that creation itself is set free from its bondage to corruption (Rom. 8:19–21). The last Adam invites us to be born again, remain in him, and bear the fruits of his Spirit in a way unlike the world has ever seen.

God is making the best use of the time. He is uniting all things in Christ—things in heaven and things on earth (Eph. 1:10). Immeasurably great power is irrevocably accomplishing all his holy will. With this power he raised Christ from the dead and seated him at his right hand in the heavenly places, far above all rule and authority and power and dominion. The name of Jesus is above every name that is named, not only in this age but also in the one to come. God put all things under Christ's feet and gave him as head over all things to the church, which is his body, the fullness of him who fills all in all (Eph. 1:19–23). Our hope is in Jesus, and someday, when his kingdom comes in full, we will not have any more of our former-world problems.

Today cannot possibly be merely another ambiguous day in which we plod for twenty-four hours only to languish in the same boredom tomorrow. No, for today we rejoice because our victorious Christ decisively defeated all his enemies, clearing them out of his way so that he might build his temple.[2] Today is a unique event filled with unfathomable opportunities to revel in the light of the kingdom that has broken into our lives. Jesus Christ, representative head for the new humanity, is seated at God's right hand—human "dust" is on the throne forever! Our

King rules us with his love as all his elect are being gathered in. Who is this King of glory? He is the Lord, strong and mighty— mighty in battle. He is *the Lord of hosts* (Ps. 24:8, 10).

As men and women and children from every tribe cling to him in their hearts by faith and become members of his royal priesthood, his temple grows and spreads all over the earth like a garden that overtakes the wasteland. Let us then proclaim the excellencies of him who called us out of darkness into his marvelous light (1 Pet. 2:9). "Through him then let us continually offer up a sacrifice of praise to God, that is, the fruit of lips that acknowledge his name" (Heb. 13:15). Let's ask him to do far more abundantly than all we ask or think according to that immeasurably great power. He will have his glory, and there is nothing on earth that any nation could desire that is more wonderful and satisfying than he. What was hidden for ages has now been revealed. Do you see the Son of Man seated far above all things? He comes to make his blessings flow far as the curse is found. Far as the curse is found. Far as the curse is found.[3]

> To him be glory in the church and in Christ Jesus throughout all generations, forever and ever. Amen. —Ephesians 3:21

Selected Bibliography

Alexander, T. Desmond. *From Eden to the New Jerusalem: An Introduction to Biblical Theology.* Grand Rapids, MI: Kregel Academic, 2008.

Beale, G. K. *A New Testament Biblical Theology: The Unfolding of the Old Testament in the New.* Grand Rapids, MI: Baker Academic, 2011.

Beale, G. K., and Mitchell Kim. *God Dwells Among Us: Expanding Eden to the Ends of the Earth.* Nottingham, UK: Inter-Varsity Press, 2014.

Bruce, F. F. *The Epistles to the Colossians, to Philemon, and to the Ephesians.* New International Commentary on the New Testament. Grand Rapids, MI: Eerdmans, 1984.

Goldsworthy, Graeme. *According to Plan: The Unfolding Revelation of God in the Bible.* Nottingham, UK: Inter-Varsity Press, 1991.

Gombis, Timothy G. *The Drama of Ephesians: Participating in the Triumph of God.* Downers Grove, IL: IVP Academic, 2010.

Lincoln, A. T. *Ephesians.* Word Biblical Commentary 42. Dallas: Word, 1990.

Mathison, Keith A. *From Age to Age: The Unfolding of Biblical Eschatology.* Phillipsburg, NJ: P&R, 2009.

Peterson, Robert A. *Salvation Accomplished by the Son: The Work of Christ.* Wheaton, IL: Crossway, 2012.

Schreiner, Thomas R. *The King in His Beauty: A Biblical Theology of the Old and New Testaments.* Grand Rapids, MI: Baker Academic, 2013.

Stott, John R. W. *The Message of Ephesians: God's New Society.* Downers Grove, IL: InterVarsity Press, 1979.

Notes

Acknowledgments

1. J. I. Packer, *Evangelism and the Sovereignty of God* (Downers Grove, IL: InterVarsity Press, 1991), 26.

Introduction

1. D. Martyn Lloyd-Jones, *God's Ultimate Purpose—An Exposition of Ephesians 1* (Grand Rapids, MI: Baker, 1978), 11–12.

2. Kevin Vanhoozer, "Gospel Theater: Staging, Scripting, Directing," the first of two lectures by Kevin Vanhoozer regarding some of the themes of his book *The Drama of Doctrine: A Canonical Linguistic Approach to Christian Doctrine* (Louisville, KY: Westminster, 2005). These lectures were given to students of Southeastern Baptist Theological Seminary in 2009. I'm grateful to Dr. Vanhoozer for his thought-provoking books, and his influence has significantly impacted the way I read Ephesians, in particular.

Chapter 1: Blessed in Christ

1. Richard Sibbes, *Glorious Freedom* (Edinburgh: Banner of Truth, 2000), 102–3.

2. John Owen, *Of the Mortification of Sin in Believers* (free from Christian Classics Ethereal Library: http://www.ccel.org/ccel/owen/mort.html).

3. G. K. Beale, *A New Testament Biblical Theology: The Unfolding of the Old Testament in the New* (Grand Rapids, MI: Baker Academic, 2011), 180–81.

4. Ibid., 763.

5. Keith A. Mathison, *From Age to Age: The Unfolding of Biblical Eschatology* (Phillipsburg, NJ: P&R, 2009), 595.

6. Justin Taylor synthesizes Michael S. Horton, *The Christian Faith: A Systematic Theology for Pilgrims on the Way* (Grand Rapids, MI: Zondervan, 2011), https://blogs.thegospelcoalition.org/justintaylor/2015/03/12/why-the -christian-narrative-is-not-a-metanarrative/, March 12, 2015, accessed August 23, 2016.

Chapter 2: Called to Hope

1. For more on this concept, please see resources from Dr. Kevin J. Vanhoozer, including his book on this theme entitled, *Faith Speaking Understanding: Performing the Drama of Doctrine* (Louisville, KY: Westminster, 2014).

2. Herman Ridderbos, *Paul and Jesus: Origin and General Character of Paul's Preaching of Christ*, trans. David H. Freeman (Grand Rapids, MI: Baker, 1958), 64–65.

3. D. M. Hay, *Glory at the Right Hand: Psalm 110 in Early Christianity* (Nashville: Abingdon, 1973), 15. There are thirty-three passages in the New Testament that quote or allude to Ps. 110:1, 4, in reference to Christ's exaltation over the powers, his position at God's right hand, his priestly office, and/or Christians being seated in the heavenly places.

4. G. K. Beale, *A New Testament Biblical Theology: The Unfolding of the Old Testament in the New* (Grand Rapids, MI: Baker Academic, 2011), 553.

5. G. K. Beale and Mitchell Kim, *God Dwells Among Us: Expanding Eden to the Ends of the Earth* (Nottingham, UK: Inter-Varsity Press, 2014), 129.

6. Tony Reinke, personal email; published with permission from the author.

Chapter 3: Zombies Raised to Life

1. John R. W. Stott, *The Message of Ephesians: God's New Society* (Downers Grove, IL: InterVarsity Press, 1979), 71.

2. Graeme Goldsworthy, *According to Plan: The Unfolding Revelation of God in the Bible* (Nottingham, UK: Inter-Varsity Press, 1991), 228.

3. Ibid., 223.

4. "One of the consistent conclusions through this section is that those who have begun to be a part of the new creation will inevitably progress and grow in this new-creational life, which means that they will grow in godly living. This is not an option. It is not something that may or may not happen. All the passages studied above (and many others) assert that true believers will necessarily and increasingly be characterized by obedience. This may happen slowly, but it will come about surely, as Eph. 2:10 asserts: 'For we are his [new] creation, created in Christ Jesus for good works, which God prepared beforehand so that we would walk in them.'" G. K. Beale, *A New Testament Biblical Theology: The Unfolding of the Old Testament in the New* (Grand Rapids, MI: Baker Academic, 2011), 865.

5. "It is this theological and anthropological outlook about the 'new man' that Paul and other NT writers use as the rhetorical basis to exhort and encourage believers on to godliness." Ibid., 849.

6. Isa. 56:6–8; 57:14–19; 66:18–21. Cited in G. K. Beale and Mitchell Kim, *God Dwells Among Us: Expanding Eden to the Ends of the Earth* (Nottingham, UK: Inter-Varsity Press, 2014), 101.

7. Beale and Kim, *God Dwells Among Us*, 104.

8. Mark Dever, "The Church Is the Gospel Made Visible," in *The (Unadjusted) Gospel* (Wheaton, IL: Crossway, 2014), 19.

Chapter 4: Mystery Revealed

1. Collin Hansen, *Blind Spots: Becoming a Courageous, Compassionate, and Commissioned Church* (Wheaton, IL: Crossway, 2015), 33.
2. John R. W. Stott, *The Message of Ephesians: God's New Society* (Downers Grove, IL: InterVarsity Press, 1979), 116.
3. Just a few other brilliant Old Testament glimpses into the mystery can be seen in Ps. 2:8 and Isa. 42:6; 49:6.
4. "So what led to Jewish opposition to Paul was his bold, uncompromising espousal of the Gentile cause. He not only preached his vision of the new and undivided humanity and wrote about it; he was at that moment suffering for the very truths he was expounding." Stott, *Message of Ephesians*, 115.
5. G. K. Beale, *The Temple and the Church's Mission: A Biblical Theology of the Dwelling Place of God* (Downers Grove, IL: IVP Academic, 2004), 259.
6. Ibid., 401.
7. Stott, *Message of Ephesians*, 120.
8. For a great read on the character of an evangelist, read Mack Stiles's book *Marks of the Messenger: Knowing, Living, and Speaking the Gospel* (Downers Grove, IL: InterVarsity Press, 2010).
9. Stott, *Message of Ephesians*, 121.
10. Tony Reinke, personal email; published with permission from the author. Reinke's book *The Joy Project: A True Story of Inescapable Happiness* (Minneapolis: Desiring God, 2015) explores the fact of God's unbounded, overflowing joy in himself. Jesus Christ is matchless in his joy, and another reason for us to worship our great God is his joy in overcoming his enemies and the way he has done so through his cross.
11. The word for manifold (*polupoikilos*) means "many colored."
12. Richard Sibbes, *Glorious Freedom* (Edinburgh: Banner of Truth, 2000), 96.
13. S. M. Baugh, note at Eph. 3:19, *The ESV Study Bible*, ed. Wayne Grudem (Wheaton, IL: Crossway, 2008), 2,267; emphasis added.
14. Stott, *Message of Ephesians*, 126. "Every church in every place at every time is in need of reform and renewal. But we need to beware lest we despise the church of God, and are blind to his work in history. We may safely say that God has not abandoned his church, however displeased with it he may be. He is still building and refining it. And if God has not abandoned it, how can we?"

Chapter 5: Walk This Way

1. John R. W. Stott, *The Message of Ephesians: God's New Society* (Downers Grove, IL: InterVarsity Press, 1979), 151.
2. Ibid.

3. See Rom. 12:6–8; 1 Cor. 12–13; Eph. 4:7–13; 1 Pet. 4:9–11.
4. G. K. Beale and Mitchell Kim, *God Dwells Among Us: Expanding Eden to the Ends of the Earth* (Nottingham, UK: Inter-Varsity Press, 2014), 106.
5. Robert A. Peterson, *Salvation Accomplished by the Son: The Work of Christ* (Wheaton, IL: Crossway, 2012), 460.
6. I'm indebted to G. K. Beale's consistent and creative exposition of the storyline of Scripture, especially in light of the temple motif. See G. K. Beale, *A New Testament Biblical Theology: The Unfolding of the Old Testament in the New* (Grand Rapids, MI: Baker Academic, 2011).

Chapter 6: Getting Real

1. F. F. Bruce, *The Epistles to the Colossians, to Philemon, and to the Ephesians*, New International Commentary on the New Testament (Grand Rapids, MI: Eerdmans, 1984), 247–48.
2. This exhortation has transformed the way I view my everyday ministry: "All believers in Christ are priests whose service reflects God's presence to others through their life and words. This reflection of God's presence in the unseen sanctuary shines light into the darkness of the world and transforms those in the darkness to reflect God's presence and become reflective images of God in his temple. This is how the temple expands throughout the church age." G. K. Beale and Mitchell Kim, *God Dwells Among Us: Expanding Eden to the Ends of the Earth* (Nottingham, UK: Inter-Varsity Press, 2014), 122.
3. G. K. Beale, *We Become What We Worship* (Downers Grove, IL: InterVarsity Press, 2008), 132.
4. Beale's work on this critical topic is quoted elsewhere in this book, and I highly recommend his volume by the same name: *We Become What We Worship*.
5. Rom. 13:12; Col. 3:8; 1 Pet. 2:1; James 1:21.
6. "If heathen degradation is due to the futility of their minds, then Christian righteousness depends on the constant renewing of our minds." John R. W. Stott, *The Message of Ephesians: God's New Society* (Downers Grove, IL: InterVarsity Press, 1979), 182.
7. William Cowper, "O for a Closer Walk with God," in Richard Conyer's *Collection of Psalms and Hymns*, 1772. For lyrics, see http://cyberhymnal.org/htm/o/f/oforaclo.htm.
8. Richard Sibbes, *Glorious Freedom* (Edinburgh: Banner of Truth, 2000), 71
9. "Paul's exhortations may be explained in terms of the indicative and imperative, which is another way of reflecting on Pauline eschatology." Thomas R. Schreiner, *The King in His Beauty: A Biblical Theology of the Old and New Testaments* (Grand Rapids, MI: Baker Academic, 2013), 565.
10. Kevin Vanhoozer, "Gospel Theater: Staging, Scripting, Directing," the first of two lectures by Kevin Vanhoozer regarding some of the themes of his book *The Drama of Doctrine: A Canonical Linguistic Approach to Christian*

Doctrine (Louisville, KY: Westminster, 2005). These lectures were given to students of Southeastern Baptist Theological Seminary in 2009.

Chapter 7: Sacrificial Love

1. "Believers are to be filled by Christ by means of the Spirit with the content of the fullness of God." Daniel B. Wallace, *Greek Grammar Beyond the Basics: An Exegetical Syntax of the New Testament with Scripture, Subject, and Greek Word Indexes* (Grand Rapids, MI: Zondervan, 1997), 375.

2. G. K. Beale, *A New Testament Biblical Theology: The Unfolding of the Old Testament in the New* (Grand Rapids, MI: Baker Academic, 2011), 940.

3. One of the books that has most impacted my thinking on this (and my life!) is *This Momentary Marriage: A Parable of Permanence* by John Piper. You can download a free PDF on the Desiring God website: http://www.desiring god.org/books/this-momentary-marriage.

4. Beale, *New Testament Biblical Theology*, 883.

5. This observation comes from Matthew Henry, *Commentary on Genesis 2:21* (1706), whom I found cited in Michael Reeves, *Christ Our Life* (Milton Keynes, UK: Paternoster, 2014), 25. Reeves's book is an outstanding treatment of the doctrine of union with Christ. I highly commend this book for its creative presentation and engaging tone.

6. Separation, divorce, and remarriage are serious issues. The Bible has much to say about them. If you are looking for help and direction in discerning wisdom in these areas, I recommend Jay E. Adams, *Marriage, Divorce, and Remarriage in the Bible* (Grand Rapids, MI: Zondervan, 1986). It is a comprehensive yet concise look at the Scripture passages that relate to these things. May I also recommend that you visit the Christian Counseling and Education Foundation website and look through their counseling resources on divorce, which are organized under the tag http://www.ccef.org/topics /divorce.

7. For more reading on these issues I recommend these helpful resources from a variety of genres: Kevin Bales, *The Slave Next Door* (Oakland, CA: University of California Press, 2008); Ben Reaoch, *Women, Slaves and the Gender Debate* (Phillipsburg, NJ: P&R, 2012); Eric Metaxas, *Amazing Grace: William Wilberforce and the Heroic Campaign to End Slavery* (New York: HarperCollins, 2009).

Chapter 8: Cruciform Armor

1. G. K. Beale and Mitchell Kim, *God Dwells Among Us: Expanding Eden to the Ends of the Earth* (Nottingham, UK: Inter-Varsity Press, 2014), 141.

2. For more on this theme, please see G. K. Beale, *The Temple in the Church's Mission: A Biblical Theology of the Dwelling Place of God* (Downers Grove, IL: IVP Academic, 2004), 63–64.

3. Isaac Watts, "Joy to the World," 1719.

General Index

accountability, 143
Adam and Eve, 30–31, 50–51, 60, 129; marriage of, 153–54; temptation of, 97
age, end of, 82
armor: clothed in, 169; cruciform, 163, 167, 170; as God's, 163; spiritual, 71, 165
armor of God, 169
"authentic Christian life," 73
authority, 148; of fathers, 158; submission to, 146–47

blessings: of Psalm 103, 26–28; spiritual, 27, 34, 97, 115
body of Christ, 79, 81, 88, 142; building of, 114; and demonic doctrine, 118–20; equality in, 150; growth of, 124; identity in, 135; local, 169; planted in, 99; work of, 103

call, 107; of Christians, 77, 79; of the church, 82; to hope, 52, 53–54; of Jesus Christ, 91
"chains," 170
Christians: adoption of, 79; all of, 48, 77, 79; as the church, 60; equality of, 150; as God's inheritance, 37; as God's temple, 80–81; inheritance of, 54; life of, 108; as light, 138; love of, 47; mission of, 40; priestly status of, 83; as saints, 26; as sojourners, 61; status of, 78; strength of, 163; transformation of, 126–27; unity of, 79–80, 90–92, 108
church, the, 57, 58–59; as bride, 155–56, 159–60, 163, 170; as building, 89; call of, 82; as Christ's bride, 61–62, 98; as God's called people, 60; God's presence in, 61; mark of, 91; mystery of, 87; as new creation, 103; as place for growth, 99; role of, 61–62; unity of, 80
cleanliness, spiritual, 35
community, garden of, 99–100, 102
Cowper, William, 136

death: power of, 56; subjected to Christ, 168
Dever, Mark, 82

Scripture Index

Also Available from Gloria Furman

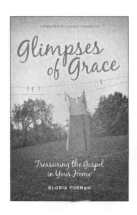

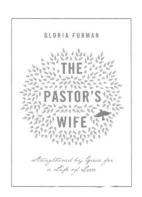

For more information, visit crossway.org.